The One-Stop Guide to Christianity

THE
ONE-STOP
Guide to
Christianity

David Winter

LION

Copyright © 2009 David Winter
This edition copyright © 2009 Lion Hudson

The author asserts the moral right
to be identified as the author of this work

A Lion Book
an imprint of
Lion Hudson plc
Wilkinson House, Jordan Hill Road,
Oxford OX2 8DR, England
www.lionhudson.com

ISBN 978 0 7459 5323 6 (UK)
ISBN 978 0 8254 7857 4 (US)

Distributed by:
UK: Marston Book Services, PO Box 269, Abingdon, Oxon, OX14 4YN
USA: Trafalgar Square Publishing, 814 N. Franklin Street, Chicago, IL 60610
USA Christian Market: Kregel Publications, PO Box 2607, Grand Rapids,
Michigan 49501

First edition 2009
10 9 8 7 6 5 4 3 2 1 0

Acknowledgments
Scripture quotations are taken from the New Revised Standard Version of the
Bible, © 1946, 1952, 1971 by the Division of Christian Education of the National
Council of Churches of Christ in the USA, and used by permission.

A catalogue record for this book is available
from the British Library

Typeset in News 702 BT and Humanist 777 BT
Printed and bound in China

Contents

Introduction

Far from dying out, religion seems to be rampant in the modern world. Most of the world's population follow one or other of the great faiths. Although it is often conflict and violence that draw attention to religious commitment, the truth is that literally billions of people find security and fulfilment in their religion, which is not for them a flag or a sword to wave but a way of life to follow.

This book is a guide to the largest of those faiths – Christianity. Alone among the world religions it is genuinely international and world-wide: there are Christian believers in every country in the world. While there have been dark periods in its history, times when it has thought that the sword is mightier than the spirit, it also has many wonderful achievements to its credit – the first orphanages, hospitals, hospices and relief agencies were Christian. The Christian church pioneered universal education. It was Christians who led the fight to abolish legalized slavery. Still today much of the educational and medical work in the world's poorest countries is carried on in Christian schools, clinics and hospitals.

This book is an introduction to Christianity – what its followers believe, and what they do. It should prove helpful to those studying the subject in school or higher education, and I hope it will also appeal to those who would like to know what it is that makes this religion so important to so many people. At the same time, there are many Christians, especially those new to their faith, who would value a clear, uncomplicated and non-technical explanation for many of the things they have been expected to take for granted. I've tried to assume little or no prior knowledge of the subject, but to present a picture of a religion which, whatever its faults and failings, has had an enormous influence on the history of the human race, the way we live our lives and the sort of people we are.

It's impossible to write about Christianity without giving first place to the figure of Jesus of Nazareth. Unlike Buddha or Confucius, for instance, it is not his teachings (wonderful as they are recognized to be) that are the heart of the Christian religion, but his life, death and resurrection from the dead. It is that weaving of events into a pattern of beliefs that makes Christianity distinctive. As we shall see, everything in the Christian story hinges on the few years of the public ministry of Jesus two thousand years ago.

Given the vastness of the subject, inevitably the picture will be incomplete. Two millennia of Christianity and a faith that follows many different traditions and even variations of belief can't be easily summed up in one volume of words and pictures. What I hope is that the picture I offer will be both fair and sufficiently detailed to present the Christian faith as it really is today, not just in theory, but in the life and experience of its followers.

Christianity

The Christian faith has as its starting point belief in God as Creator – a belief shared, of course, by Jews and Muslims. However, Christianity gives a central place to the life of Jesus of Nazareth, a prophet and healer who was born in Bethlehem in around 4 BCE, in the Roman province of Judea, and who grew up in his parental home at Nazareth in Galilee. At about the age of 30 he began a remarkable public ministry of preaching and healing, eventually being arrested by the Jewish religious authorities on charges of blasphemy and executed by crucifixion under the Roman prefect Pontius Pilate. On the third day after his death and burial, his followers claimed that he had risen from the dead and that they had seen him and talked with him. Several of them died rather than withdraw this claim. Within two or three decades there were Christian believers in many parts of the Roman empire, including the imperial capital, Rome.

Telling the Christian Story

There are four 'Gospels', literally 'Good News' books, which each tell in their own way the story of Jesus.

Mark is the earliest and shortest, probably written between 65 and 70 CE. There is evidence that the apostle Peter may have been a source for some of his material.

Matthew is placed first among the Gospels, probably because his intention is to link the story of Jesus to what had gone before in the history of the Jewish people. His Gospel is usually dated around 80 CE.

Luke is the only Gospel written by a Gentile. He was a medical doctor and a companion and friend of the apostle Paul. His Gospel was probably written between 70 and 75 CE.

John is the 'odd one out' among the Gospels – very different in style, though telling basically the same story. The author (or source) claims to have been an eye-witness of the events he relates. This book seems to be a reflection of the impact Jesus made on the lives of those closest to him, but written some time after the event, probably about 95 CE.

The apostle Paul also gives us the earliest written evidence of the words and actions of Jesus in his account of the institution of the last supper (1 Corinthians 11:23–26). Written in about 55 CE – about 22 years after the crucifixion of Jesus – this is the earliest record we have of the event.

The Torah Scroll from which the Daily Chapter is read in the synagogue.

Four Christian Beliefs

God as Creator: He is the origin and source of everything that exists, and he gives it meaning and purpose.

People: Human beings are made 'in the image of God' and are consequently of infinite value.

Redeemer: Despite being made in God's image, human beings have consistently failed to live as God requires. They need to be rescued from the situation they have created for themselves. God sent a Redeemer, Jesus, to achieve this.

Spirit: God is at work in the world, and in people's lives, through the Holy Spirit, the 'special helper' sent by God after Jesus left the earth.

Key People

Abraham was the 'father' of the Hebrew tribes and indeed of all Semitic peoples. Prompted by God, he migrated from Ur of the Chaldees (in modern Iraq), probably in the second millennium BCE, to Canaan. He was told by God that he would be the father of a great people, through whom all the nations of the earth would be blessed.

Moses led the Hebrews out of slavery in Egypt to the border of the promised land, Canaan, in the late second millennium BCE. At Mount Sinai he received the Law from God, including the Ten Commandments.

Isaiah was a prophet in the eighth and seventh centuries BCE who foretold the coming of a great deliverer who would bring blessing to Israel and to the whole world.

John the Baptist was a contemporary of Jesus. He described himself as the 'voice' prophesied by Isaiah who would call people to be ready for the coming of the Messiah, God's anointed deliverer. He spoke of one coming after him who would be far greater than him, and identified Jesus as that person.

Jesus of Nazareth was the son of Mary who was married to the carpenter Joseph. His probable dates were 4 BCE–30 or 32 CE.

Paul was an early convert to Christianity who preached and planted churches around the eastern Mediterranean and whose letters form part of the New Testament.

Peter was the leader of the twelve 'apostles', the 'special messengers' of Jesus. He was the first to preach the Christian gospel to the Jews, on the Day of Pentecost, and to Gentiles, in the house of Cornelius (see Acts 2 and 10).

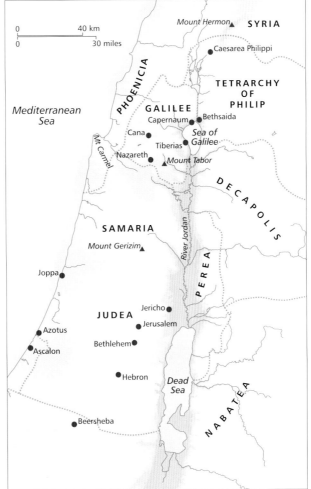

Palestine at the time of Jesus.

THE EARLIEST CREED

From early days the Christian faith was summarized in simple 'creeds' (statements of belief), especially for the benefit of those new converts being prepared for baptism. Here is one of the earliest:

'Do you believe in Christ Jesus, the Son of God, who was born of the Holy Spirit of the Virgin Mary, and was crucified under Pontius Pilate, and was dead and buried, and rose again the third day, alive from the dead, and ascended into heaven, and sat at the right hand of the Father, and will come to judge the living and the dead?'
HIPPOLYTUS, THIRD CENTURY CE

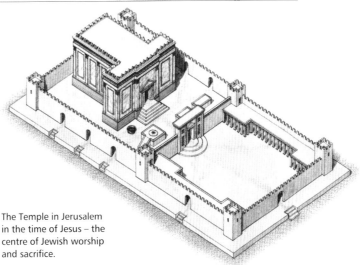

The Temple in Jerusalem in the time of Jesus – the centre of Jewish worship and sacrifice.

Where Did It Come From?
THE ORIGINS OF CHRISTIANITY

Christianity is a child of Judaism, the religion of the Jewish people. In fact, it is difficult, if not impossible, to understand the Christian faith without recognizing its Jewish roots. Jesus was a Jew. His Scriptures were the Hebrew Bible. All of his 'apostles' were Jews and so were the first three thousand converts. Jesus himself said that he had not come to abolish the Law of Moses or the teachings of the Hebrew prophets, but to fulfil them.

However, the faith soon began to make inroads into the Greek and Roman worlds and a large number of those converting to Christianity were Gentiles, so the young church and the synagogues were set on a collision course. For several centuries there was fierce and often bitter confrontation between the two, and subsequently – shamefully – the Christian church from time to time engaged in organized massacres of Jews ('pogroms'), especially in Russia and eastern Europe. Happily, in the modern era Christians have come to acknowledge their historic debt to Judaism and the two faiths generally live side by side in mutual respect and understanding.

YAHWEH: 'I AM'

Many ideas were summed up in the name by which the Hebrews came to know God: *Yahweh*. It is the most common pronoun in the Hebrew Scriptures (used 6,000 times), yet it doesn't appear as such even once in most of our Bibles. However, when the LORD is spelt in capital letters, that means that the holy name, *Yahweh*, is being used.

The name *Yahweh* is probably based on the Hebrew verb 'to be' – God simply exists, he can call himself 'I Am'. The 'God of Abraham, Isaac and Jacob' is the one, true, everlasting, invisible personal God. And he, for Christians, is the Father of Jesus Christ.

The One, True God

The story of the Hebrew Scriptures (what Christians call the 'Old Testament') is of a slowly unfolding revelation of the nature of the one God. Slowly, over many centuries, the Jewish people came to understand that 'their' God was the God of the whole creation.

THE GOD OF THE WHOLE EARTH

Abraham, Moses, David, Elijah, Isaiah, Ezekiel – these, and many others, contributed to this process. They wrestled with the mystery of a God who was both the God of Israel and the God of the whole earth, who was infinite (without beginning or end), personal (not an idol or the sun or the local mountain) and good (not cruel, arbitrary or merciless).

The Jewish religion (Judaism) was born in the land between the Syrian desert and the Mediterranean Sea.

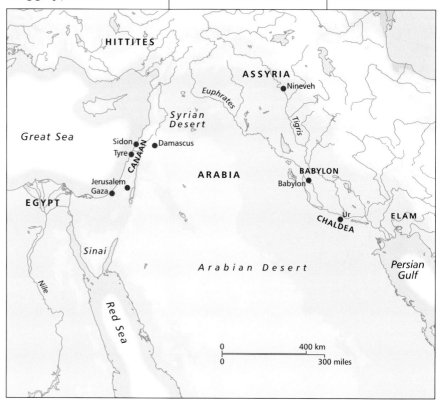

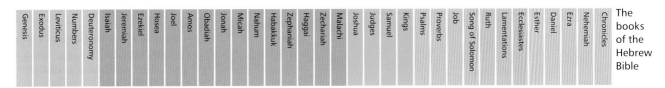

Genesis | Exodus | Leviticus | Numbers | Deuteronomy | Isaiah | Jeremiah | Ezekiel | Hosea | Joel | Amos | Obadiah | Jonah | Micah | Nahum | Habakkuk | Zephaniah | Haggai | Zechariah | Malachi | Joshua | Judges | Samuel | Kings | Psalms | Proverbs | Job | Song of Solomon | Ruth | Lamentations | Ecclesiastes | Esther | Daniel | Ezra | Nehemiah | Chronicles

The books of the Hebrew Bible

The Books of the Old Testament

The Law (the Pentateuch): Genesis, Exodus, Leviticus, Numbers, Deuteronomy

The Prophets: Isaiah, Jeremiah, Ezekiel, Hosea, Joel, Amos, Obadiah, Jonah, Micah, Nahum, Habakkuk, Zephaniah, Haggai, Zechariah, Malachi

The Writings (historical): Joshua, Judges, Samuel, Kings

The Writings (wisdom): Psalms, Proverbs, Job, Song of Solomon, Ruth, Lamentations, Ecclesiastes

Other books: Esther, Daniel, Ezra, Nehemiah, Chronicles

The Hebrew Scriptures

The books of the 'Old Testament' have six main messages to convey:

1. God is the Creator

2. God values what he has made

3. He revealed himself to the Hebrew people (Israel)

4. He gave them a moral code (the Law)

5. They failed to do what he required

6. God will send an anointed Saviour, the 'Messiah'

Key Themes in the Old Testament

God as Creator

It is he that made us, and we are his; we are his people, and the sheep of his pasture.
PSALM 100:3

God as Law-giver

Happy are those who do not follow the advice of the wicked, or take the path that sinners tread, or sit in the seat of scoffers; but their delight is in the law of the LORD, and on his law they meditate day and night.
PSALM 1:1, 2

God as Judge

For not from the east or from the west and not from the wilderness comes lifting up; but it is God who executes judgment, putting down one and lifting up another.
PSALM 75:6,7

God of Truth

The sum of your word is truth; and every one of your righteous ordinances endures for ever.
PSALM 119:160

The synagogue, the place of Jewish worship and teaching. This example is at Fez, Morocco.

God of Mercy and Love

The LORD is merciful and gracious, slow to anger and abounding in steadfast love.

He will not always accuse, nor will he keep his anger for ever.

He does not deal with us according to our sins, nor repay us according to our iniquities.

For as the heavens are high above the earth, so great is his steadfast love toward those who fear him.
PSALM 103:8-11

AN UNFINISHED REVELATION

In the very last book of the Hebrew Scriptures, the prophet Malachi tells his Jewish readers that 'the Lord whom you seek will suddenly come to his temple' (Malachi 3:1). So the revelation is unfinished. There is more to come – indeed, as Malachi goes on to prophesy, there will be a period of purifying and testing leading eventually to a time of rich blessing.

For Christians the revelation of God in the Old Testament is only complete when he has revealed himself in his Son, Jesus. He is the human face of the invisible God, the 'Word made flesh' (John 1:14).

11

The Bible

THE PEOPLE OF THE BOOK

There are two objects that you can find in almost any church the world over – a table and a book. The table (often called the 'altar') is for celebrating the Holy Communion; the book, the Bible, is for public reading in services.

Every Christian church acknowledges the authority of the Bible as a primary source of doctrine. Many churches make it their sole authority for matters of faith.

Probably more important is the place that the Bible has in the life of the church. In many churches it is read in every service and preached on in sermons and homilies, and it is often read at home and reflected on by 'ordinary' Christians. Its teaching, stories, sermons, songs and visions are the life-blood of the church. Christians are 'the people of the book'.

The Bible stands in an honoured place in church. This example is in Lancing College Chapel, Sussex, England.

Who Wrote It?

The Bible is the work of many different authors, some of whom remain anonymous, written over a period of at least a thousand years. The first part of the Bible is known as the 'Old Testament'. Its first five books are called the 'books of Moses', but he couldn't have written all of them because the last book records his death. The longest historical books (Kings and Chronicles) were written by anonymous chroniclers and were subsequently edited and revised by later scribes. The Psalms are often called 'The Psalms of David', but it's most unlikely that he wrote all, or even most, of them. The books of the prophets each have a name given to them, but whether the prophet himself or a convenient scribe actually recorded his sayings and actions we can't tell.

When it comes to the second part of the Bible, the New Testament, we have more evidence to help us, and we can be fairly sure who wrote most of it – indeed, two men, Luke and Paul, account for more than half of it!

Who Says?

Who says any particular piece of writing should be part of the 'Bible'?

The Hebrew Scriptures (the 'Old Testament') were finally brought together as a collection of sacred writings in the fifth and sixth centuries BCE. The Old Testament as we have it now was almost exactly the 'Scriptures' that Jesus and the first Christians knew. These Scriptures were regarded by Jews as embodying the 'word of the Lord', in the Law and the Prophets.

The New Testament was built around the Gospels, with their accounts of the life and death of Jesus, and the letters of the apostles. By the second century they were regarded as being on a par with the Hebrew Scriptures (see 2 Peter 3:16) and they were eventually recognized as the Christian Scriptures by the Councils of the Church in the fifth century CE.

THE OLD TESTAMENT (THE HEBREW SCRIPTURES)

The Books of Moses (the Decalogue)   The Historical Books   The Wisdom Books   The Prophets

Genesis · Exodus · Leviticus · Numbers · Deuteronomy · Joshua · Judges · Ruth · 1 Samuel · 2 Samuel · 1 Kings · 2 Kings · 1 Chronicles · 2 Chronicles · Ezra · Nehemiah · Esther · Job · Psalms · Proverbs · Ecclesiastes · Song of Songs · Isaiah · Jeremiah · Lamentations · Ezekiel · Daniel · Hosea · Joel · Amos · Obadiah · Jonah · Micah · Nahum · Habakkuk · Zephaniah · Haggai · Zechariah · Malachi

True or False?

How do we know that what we have now in our Bibles is what was originally written? And how sure can we be that the Gospels, for instance, are accurate records of the life of Jesus?

The answer to the first question is simply that the sacred writings were regarded with such reverence and respect that they were copied and handed down with meticulous attention over the centuries. When the Dead Sea Scrolls were discovered in 1947, providing us with texts of the Hebrew Scriptures from hundreds of years earlier than anything previously available, the differences were marginal. The scribes had done their job well!

The caves where the Dead Sea Scrolls were found.

Where the New Testament is concerned, probably all of it was written within 60 years of the events it describes. Paul's earlier letters were written a mere 23 years or so after the crucifixion of Jesus, well within the lifetime of many eye-witnesses of the events. The earliest Gospel, Mark, was written about 30 years after the events, probably by someone who was a young man at the time of the crucifixion and who was living in Jerusalem.

The Gospel writers were not neutral observers, of course! They were out to persuade their readers that Jesus rose from the dead. But were they liars? Or do their books have the ring of truth? The reader must decide.

Why Read the Bible?

1. Because it is one of the most influential books ever written.

2. Because it describes the human search for God, and God's search for us.

3. Because of its powerful influence on the lives of so many people.

4. Because it records the words and actions of Jesus.

5. Because of the vision it offers us of a world of justice and peace.

Translation

The Old Testament was mostly written in Hebrew, and the New Testament in Greek. This means that most people have to read the Bible in a translation. Largely through the work of organizations such as the Bible societies and Wycliffe Bible Translators, the

Scriptures are now available in all of the world's major languages, though many tribal languages and those spoken by minority racial groups do not yet have the Bible in their own mother tongues.

Copying the Bible – a Torah scribe at work.

WILLIAM TYNDALE

Tyndale lived during the early years of the Reformation – he was ordained in 1521 – and shared many of the Reformers' views, especially on the right of every Christian to have access to the Scriptures in their own language. He believed that 'the boy who drove the plough' should know as much about the Bible as the bishops! He set himself to translate the New Testament into English, but was forced to base himself in Germany and the Netherlands due to opposition from church leaders in England. His translation was published in 1526 and immediately denounced by the church authorities. He was arrested in the Netherlands and executed for heresy in 1536. However, his work, including a translation of much of the Old Testament, became the basis of many subsequent versions of the Bible that were freely and widely used.

THE NEW TESTAMENT (THE CHRISTIAN SCRIPTURES)

The Gospels   Acts   The Letters   Revelation

| Matthew | Mark | Luke | John | Acts | Romans | 1 Corinthians | 2 Corinthians | Galatians | Ephesians | Philippians | Colossians | 1 Thessalonians | 2 Thessalonians | 1 Timothy | 2 Timothy | Titus | Philemon | Hebrews | James | 1 Peter | 2 Peter | 1 John | 2 John | 3 John | Jude | Revelation |

The Creation and the Creator
'IN THE BEGINNING...'

To say, as Christians do, that God is the source and origin of everything that exists is to express a belief that we live in a certain kind of universe. It's not an accident. It's not random. It's not solely the product of chemical or cosmic processes. It's not without meaning and purpose. Christians believe that we live in a creation, designed by a Creator, which means that they view the universe not simply with curiosity, questions and scientific analysis, but with awe.

The first book of the Bible, Genesis, starts with a story about the creation of the stars and planets, of light and darkness, of land and water, of plants and fish, birds and animals. Finally, as the crown of the creation, God made men and women 'in his own image' (Genesis 1:27). This doesn't mean that we 'look like' God (who is Spirit, and has no bodily form) but that we share his chief characteristics: personality, self-consciousness, creativity, moral awareness. We are not clever computers linked to a physical body, but spiritual beings.

God

The Bible teaches that God is:

Eternal – he has no beginning or ending *Exodus 3:14*

Omniscient – he knows everything *2 Chronicles 16:9*

Omnipotent – there is nothing he cannot do *Jeremiah 10:12*

Personal – not an abstract power *Exodus 3:15*

Spirit – not flesh and blood *John 4:24*

Just – scrupulously fair *Genesis 18:25*

Merciful – patient and slow to judge *Numbers 14:18*

Good – in an absolute sense *1 John 1:5*

Love – the one who made us, loves us *1 John 4:8*

God gives life to Adam – Michelangelo's painting from the Sistine Chapel, Rome.

The Trinity

Christians are 'monotheists' – they believe that there is one God, but that within that one God there are three 'Persons': the Father, the Son and the Holy Spirit.

The Father is the Creator, who directs the actions of the Trinity.

The Son is the Saviour, sent by the Father to rescue the human race.

The Holy Spirit carries out the will of the Trinity, and is constantly at work in people and in the world.

Thus the one God is not a simple unity but, like many of the building blocks of the universe he created, a dynamic relationship within a complex unity. (Think of neutrons, protons and electrons!)

What People Have Said About God

'It is the heart which experiences God, and not the reason.'
BLAISE PASCAL, *PENSÉES*

'God is the indwelling and not the transient cause of all.'
BARUCH SPINOZA, *ETHICS*

'The certainty of a God giving meaning to life far surpasses in attractiveness the ability to behave badly with impunity.'
ALBERT CAMUS, *THE ABSURD MAN*

'God is the expression of the intelligent universe.'
KAHLIL GIBRAN, *VISION*

'We need God, not in order to understand the why, but to feel and sustain the ultimate wherefore, to give a meaning to the Universe.'
MIGUEL DE UNAMUNG, *LOVE, PITY, SUFFERING AND PERSONALITY*

The Genesis Creation Story

Light
(DAY ONE)

Sky and sea
(DAY TWO)

Vegetation
(DAY THREE)

Sun and moon
(DAY FOUR)

Fish, birds and reptiles
(DAY FIVE)

Humankind
(DAY SIX)

The creation of the world, from the late twelfth-century Souvigny Bible, Moulins, France.

The Garden of Eden

In the Genesis creation story, the man is set in a very beautiful and fruitful garden, called Eden. This was a 'Garden of Delights', a place of ultimate pleasure and fulfilment – a 'paradise', in fact. The man was to care for it and enjoy its fruit – but God commanded him not to eat the fruit of one tree, the 'Tree of the Knowledge of Good and Evil', which stood in the middle of the garden. To meet his need for a companion the man was given a wife. Together, they broke this simple rule and as punishment they were expelled from the garden. Only then does the Bible give them the names by which we know them – Adam (which simply means 'man') and Eve (which means 'life'). The sin of Adam and Eve was not sex, as many people seem to think, but acting as though they knew better than their Creator. This first act of human disobedience is known as 'the Fall'.

The Garden of Eden – the place of innocence – as painted on a wall in a Swiss village.

THIS BIG BANG WORLD

'I look forward to the day when it will be generally recognized that one can take on board all the deep truths of the Genesis creation stories, and, in addition, the scientific truths about God's world. Then we shall see how God is revealing himself through this Big Bang world of ours. He is actually speaking to us through these scientific discoveries.'
PROFESSOR RUSSELL STANNARD, *DOING AWAY WITH GOD?*

Sin and Forgiveness
GETTING THINGS WRONG

'Sin' is not a word used much in the modern world. People used to accuse Christians of 'going on about sin', but the truth is that many Christians seem to be as reluctant to use the term as everyone else. This is largely because of the way it has been associated primarily with certain kinds of behaviour – usually sexual – rather than being applied, as it should be, to all behaviour that is unacceptable to God.

Sin, according to the New Testament, is 'missing the mark' – falling short of what God requires (Romans 1:23). Another word the Bible uses for sin conveys the idea of 'lawlessness' (2 Corinthians 6:14) and moral depravity (1 John 3:12). Sin, in short, is behaving as though we can do what we like without reference to God, which is why idolatry – not giving God first place – is regarded as the worst possible sin (Romans 1:23).

The moment that Joseph reveals his identity to his brothers and forgives them is captured in this painting by François Gerard.

The Mount of Temptation in the Wilderness of Judea near Jericho. This is the traditional site where the devil tempted Jesus. On the mountaintop are the ruins of an early Byzantine church.

Putting Things Right

Because sin damages our relationships – with God, and with one another – forgiveness is its necessary antidote. All sin is at heart sin against God, and needs his forgiveness; but much of our sin also needs the forgiveness of those we have wronged. So the idea of forgiveness is much more easily accepted by people than the idea of sin: we would all like to be forgiven, and sometimes we can even be persuaded to forgive!

All through the Bible God is seen as a Father who forgives – sometimes individuals, sometimes the whole people of Israel. This forgiveness cannot be earned; it is an act of his own free will, a demonstration of his 'steadfast love' (Psalm 51:1). When God forgives a sin, he also forgets it (Jeremiah 31:34). In the Gospels, Jesus both offered forgiveness to people, and called his followers to forgive those who had wronged them. As the Lord's Prayer says, 'Forgive us our sins, as we forgive those who sin against us' (Luke 11:4).

Great Acts of Forgiveness

Joseph (the one with the technicoloured dreamcoat) forgave his envious brothers for selling him off as a slave (Genesis 45:4–13).

The Lord forgave King David for committing adultery with Bathsheba and then murdering her husband Uriah (2 Samuel 12:13) – though he had to live with the consequences of his sin.

Jesus forgave the soldiers who crucified him (Luke 23:34).

Stephen, the first Christian martyr, forgave those who stoned him to death (Acts 7:60).

Sin and the Cross of Jesus

While it is true that throughout history God has been willing to forgive individuals and communities when the conditions are right, Christians believe that through the death of Jesus on the cross a more universal kind of forgiveness is now available. John the Baptist described Jesus as 'the Lamb of God, who takes away the sin of the world' (John 1:29). This is different from the forgiveness of individual or even corporate sins. Through his death Jesus dealt with the whole principle of sin – it was a cosmic act of forgiveness. The apostle Paul describes it as removing the powerful 'sting' of sin (1 Corinthians 15:56). From that moment on, the deadly grip of sin on the human race was broken and a new way of living was opened up for those who turned to Christ.

The Seven Deadly Sins

And their contrary virtues

Pride	Humility
Anger	Kindness
Lust	Self-control
Greed	Generosity
Envy	Love
Sloth	Zeal
Gluttony	Temperance

These sins and virtues are not listed in this way in the Bible, but they can be brought together from several different lists, especially in the letters of Paul (see, for instance, Galatians 5:19–21 and Romans 1:29–31 for 'sins' and Galatians 5:22, 23 for contrary virtues).

'Repentance'

The normal condition for forgiveness by God is 'repentance' (see, for example, Acts 2:38). To repent is to experience a radical change of thinking, from arguing our innocence or offering excuses for our behaviour to agreeing with God that it was wrong and requires forgiveness. If we are prepared to do that, God is true to his promise and will forgive us our sins (see 1 John 1:9).

Sayings About Sin

Be sure your sin will find you out.
NUMBERS 32:23

'Between these two, the denying of sins we have done, and the bragging of sins we have not done, what a space, what a compass is there for millions and millions of sins!'
JOHN DONNE, *SERMONS NO 2*

'People are no longer sinful, they are only immature or under-privileged or frightened, or more particularly, sick.'
PHYLLIS MCGINLEY, *IN DEFENSE OF SIN*

'Sins cannot be undone, only forgiven.'
IGOR STRAVINSKY, *CONVERSATIONS*

DESMOND TUTU

When South Africa finally achieved a multi-racial government after the elections of 1994, President Mandela appointed Desmond Tutu, the retired Archbishop of Cape Town, as chairman of what was called the 'Truth and Reconciliation Commission'. Its aim was to heal the bitter divisions that had been caused by the long years of apartheid in South Africa by bringing together the former oppressors and their victims and inviting them to seek reconciliation by facing the truth about their behaviour. Tutu counselled forgiveness and cooperation rather than revenge. Many moving stories came from the Commission, with expressions of regret and repentance from one side and of forgiveness from the other. It played a major part in the astonishing transition of South Africa from racial division to a 'Rainbow Nation'.

Modern-day Samaritans celebrate the Passover ceremony. The fire is used to burn the 'unclean' parts of the lamb.

The Cross

Most of the great world religions have some distinguishing symbol – the Qur'an, for instance, or the Star of David, a statue of the Buddha or the Sikh Scriptures. But the universal symbol of Christianity is incongruously different – it's the cross on which Jesus was executed as a criminal. This crude and repulsive means of execution now stands in tens of thousands of churches as a revered ornament, and is hung around millions of necks as a piece of religious identification. It was in fact a wooden cross on which Jesus died, put to death for blasphemy (according to the religious leaders) and threatening public stability (in the sight of the Roman occupying power).

He undoubtedly died – no one survived crucifixion; the Romans always made sure that the victim was dead. Yet on the third day after his burial the friends of Jesus found his tomb empty and the body gone. Then they started to meet him again: in the garden where he had been buried, on the road to Emmaus, in a room in Jerusalem, by a lake in Galilee. They became utterly convinced that he was alive, that God had raised him from the dead – and many of them were themselves willing to die for that belief.

Those three days changed the lives of the disciples. They changed the way in which we understand death and eternal life. They changed history, because within a few decades the belief that Jesus died and rose again was widespread throughout the Roman empire, and eventually the emperor Constantine himself became a Christian. It would be no more than the truth to say that those three days changed the world.

Why Did Jesus Die?

Humanly speaking, Jesus died because he had many powerful enemies in high places. However, from the beginning of his ministry it was clear that he believed his role was not to restore political freedom to Israel or re-establish the royal line, but to be the 'Suffering Servant of the Lord' whom Isaiah wrote about (Isaiah 53:1–10). This was his model of what it meant to be the Messiah, and he constantly told his disciples that he would be put to death, giving his life as a 'ransom' (price of freedom) for many (Mark 10:45). The constant message of the New Testament is that the death of Jesus on the cross was 'for us', 'for the forgiveness of sins'. In that sense, it was not a tragedy, but a massive victory over evil.

Jesus was put to death on a small rocky outcrop just outside the walls of Jerusalem (as they were situated at that time). Because of its appearance it was known in Aramaic as 'Golgotha', the Place of the Skull ('Calvary', in Latin).

Characters in the Story

Jesus, having spent most of his public ministry in Galilee, his home country, finally headed to Jerusalem with his disciples. He knew that the religious authorities there regarded him as a serious threat to their own position and some undoubtedly also believed that he was guilty of blasphemy for claiming divine powers. On the Thursday night after his arrival in the city, and just before the feast of the Passover, he was arrested by the Temple guards and charged with blasphemy.

Caiaphas was high priest in Jerusalem from 18 to 37 CE. He held office by permission of the Roman prefect, and as a member of the Sanhedrin, the Jewish Council, he was anxious not to disturb the uneasy compromise that allowed the Jews to have a degree of religious freedom. They felt Jesus was threatening this arrangement and handed him over to the Romans in the hope that they would agree to his execution.

Pontius Pilate was Roman prefect, or 'governor', of the province of Judaea from 26 to 37 CE. He held anti-Semitic views and despised the Jewish leaders. When faced with their request for the execution of Jesus, he at first opposed the idea but eventually gave in, fearing mass disorder. A brutal administrator, he was eventually recalled to Rome to face charges of cruelty in Samaria.

Joseph of Arimathea was a wealthy Jew, a member of the Jewish Council and a secret disciple of Jesus. He asked Pilate for the body of Jesus and laid it in a private tomb near the place of execution.

Mary Magdalene, one of the disciples of Jesus, was the first person to meet the risen Jesus, in the garden near his tomb.

Mary, the mother of Jesus, stood near the cross while her son was being crucified. He spoke from the cross, commanding John to care for his mother.

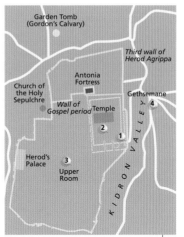

THE JOURNEY TO THE CROSS

The journey began one week before Easter Sunday when Jesus rode into Jerusalem (1) and overturned the tables of the moneychangers in the temple court (2). During the week he taught about the destruction of Jerusalem and its temple. On Thursday evening he celebrated the Passover with his disciples in a house in the city (3). Later that evening he was arrested in Gethsemane (4). Tried before the Jewish elders and then sent to the Roman governor for his death sentence to be ratified, he was crucified, probably on the site of the present Church of the Holy Sepulchre.

THE GARDEN TOMB

Visitors to Jerusalem can see a garden tomb similar to the one in which Jesus was buried at the site of what is known as 'Gordon's Calvary'. This tomb dates from the same period and is set in a garden with a wine-press. Although now outside the present walls of the city, it would have been inside them in the first century, which means that it cannot be the site of Calvary (Golgotha); that is almost certainly under the Church of the Holy Sepulchre, where a rock-tomb can be found. This site would have been outside the city walls in the time of Christ – executions always took place outside the city precincts.

Evidence for the Resurrection of Jesus

Is there any convincing evidence for the resurrection of Jesus, or is it just a matter of faith? Here are some of the factors that have convinced millions of people down the centuries that it actually happened.

The Empty Tomb: The disciples found the tomb of Jesus empty on that Sunday morning. If it was not empty, then surely the authorities would have produced the body of Jesus to silence these claims. If it was empty, then either the disciples or tomb robbers had moved the body. The first is plainly a ridiculous idea, requiring a deception that would have to be maintained for decades in the face of persecution and torture. The second is unlikely, because there was nothing of value with the body, and even the shroud was left in the tomb.

The Witness of the Disciples: The apostle Paul visited Jerusalem in 35 CE, a mere three years after the resurrection, to meet with Peter and other leaders of the church. It is inconceivable that he did not ask them about the appearances of the risen Jesus. He probably visited the tomb. About 20 years later, writing to the church at Corinth, he provides the earliest record we have of the beliefs of the first Christians. He claims that the risen Jesus appeared at different times to all the apostles and to no fewer than 500 people at once (1 Corinthians 15:6). It is probable that many of the first witnesses, young men and women at the time of the appearances, would still have been available for cross-examination. If this was mass delusion, then it was on an unprecedented scale!

The Gospel Accounts: Matthew, Mark, Luke and John all record the claim that Jesus rose from the dead and appeared to his followers over a period of some weeks. Their accounts are not identical (which rules out collusion), but they all tell fundamentally the same story. There was no shortage of clever, articulate and powerful opponents of the emerging Christian movement who would surely have seized on any evidence to disprove their claims, but there is no record at all of any convincing refutation of them.

Heaven and Hell

DESTINATIONS

'Heaven' is up above, and on the whole quite nice, if a bit religious. 'Hell' is down below, and not very nice, though pleasantly warm. That's probably how most people think of heaven and hell, if indeed they bother to think about them at all. There are plenty of jokes about them – St Peter at the pearly gates, and so on – but many people today assume that everybody goes to heaven eventually, if they go anywhere.

Christian teaching tends to think of heaven and hell as two destinations, or perhaps destinies. Heaven is the 'place' where God dwells, or a state of existence in which the will of God is perfectly done and all can live in joy and peace – the 'kingdom of heaven' that Jesus talked about. Hell, on the other hand, is a state of existence in which God is absent, and as God is the source of life and love, that suggests a very barren and desolate state of being. The Bible is quite clear that God doesn't want *anyone* to end up there – he does 'not want any to perish but all to come to repentance' (2 Peter 3:9).

The author C. S. Lewis, who wrote several books about heaven and hell.

What People Have Said About Heaven

'Heaven will be the endless portion of every man who has heaven in his soul.'
HENRY WARD BEECHER

'To believe in heaven is not to run away from life; it is to run towards it.'
JOSEPH D. BLINCO

'All the way to heaven is heaven.'
ST CATHERINE OF SIENA

'The main object of religion is not to get a man into heaven, but to get heaven into him.'
THOMAS HARDY

'Heaven means to be one with God.'
CONFUCIUS

'A man's reach should exceed his grasp, or what's a heaven for?'
ROBERT BROWNING

'I prefer to live by the faith that the kingdoms of this world shall become the kingdoms of our Lord and of his Christ, and he shall reign for ever and ever. Hallelujah!'
MARTIN LUTHER KING

Civil rights leader Martin Luther King during the 'March on Washington', August 1963.

What People Have Said About Hell

'Hell is the enjoyment of your own way forever.'
DANTE ALIGHIERI

'What is hell?... The suffering that comes from the consciousness that one is no longer able to love.'
FYODOR DOSTOEVSKY

'Heaven would be hell for an irreligious man.'
J. H. NEWMAN

'The safest road to hell is the gradual one – the gentle slope, soft underfoot, without sudden turnings, without milestones, without signposts.'
C. S. LEWIS

'There is nobody who will go to hell for company.'
GEORGE HERBERT

● SEE ALSO
LIFE AFTER DEATH P22-23
WHAT IS HEAVEN LIKE? P55

What is Heaven?

The word 'heaven' (or 'heavens') is used in the Bible to describe both the sky – the 'firmament' that the psalmist sings about – and the particular place where God dwells. Generally in the New Testament, however, it signifies a state of being where all can live in joy and peace in the presence of God and Jesus.

Jesus described it as a 'place' and said that it contains many 'dwelling-places' (John 14:2) – indeed, he promised that he would prepare a 'place' for his disciples. This suggests a great deal more than some land of shadowy spirits! All the pictures of heaven in the Bible (and they *are* pictures, not literal descriptions) are of a place of ultimate fulfilment, beauty, peace and harmony.

WHO GOES TO HEAVEN?

The answer is surprisingly simple: God knows, and nobody else! That's because only God can read our hearts, knows all about us and fully understands the circumstances of our lives and the influences that have shaped them. He has deputed the 'judgment' that decides our destiny to Jesus, so the world will be judged by the world's Saviour, which, as the apostle Paul says, is 'good news' (see Romans 2:16).

The Garden of Earthly Delights by Hieronymus Bosch. The first panel of the triptych shows Adam and Eve in Eden, and the third one the punishments of hell.

WHO GOES TO HELL?

As we have seen, nobody, if God had his way with human beings! However, if there are those who in the face of God's mercy and love persist in wilful disobedience and evil, then they will join the 'devil and his angels' in the 'lake of fire' (to use the vivid language of Revelation 20:10, 15). Again, as in the sayings of Jesus, the language is of cleansing and purification rather than punishment. God's perfect creation has been polluted, and heaven would not be heaven if things were left as they are.

What is Hell?

This question is not easily answered, because several completely different ideas in the Bible are sometimes translated by the English word 'hell'. The Hebrew *sheol* and the Greek *hades* are both translated as 'hell' in older versions of the Bible and in the old version of the Christian Creed ('he descended into hell'). In fact, they simply mean the abode of the dead, with no notion of punishment, judgment or suffering.

Jesus spoke of a place of cleansing and purification, using an Aramaic word, *Gehenna*, which referred to the dump outside Jerusalem, where rubbish was burnt in a continuous fire. Such a place, he said, would be the destiny of those who by deliberate choice did what they knew to be wrong (Mark 9:42–48).

Life After Death
HERE AND HEREAFTER

Christians believe that there is life beyond death. Jesus taught it and argued it against contemporary opponents who thought it was a daft idea. The apostles believed and taught it, and down the ages Christians have lived with one eye on eternity – the 'eternal life' that Jesus promised.

This belief was ridiculed by the Communists as 'pie in the sky when you die', an excuse for the church to ignore the very real sufferings of people on earth by promising them better things in heaven. In fact, it has been those people who believed in life after death who have done most throughout history to improve the lives of people before death, from the Franciscans and Poor Clares of the Middle Ages, who ministered to the hungry and destitute, to Mother Teresa of Calcutta and Martin Luther King, who fought the battle for the weak and powerless in the modern world.

The apostle Paul said that 'if for this life only we have hoped in Christ, we are of all people most to be pitied' (1 Corinthians 15:19). The Christian hope was, and is, that on earth we may encounter the love of God and after death we may know and enjoy him for ever.

Evidence for Life After Death

Universal Sense: Despite the evidence of our own eyes (death is all around us), most human beings throughout history seem to have believed in some kind of life beyond death. This has included many of the world's wisest men and women.

Personal Experience: Many people who have lost a loved one are convinced that in some way they are still 'alive'. Sometimes they will speak of experiences that have reinforced this belief.

'Love Never Ends': This saying of the apostle Paul (1 Corinthians 13:8) is part of his argument that love, which is the very nature of God, is eternal. It seems to follow that the love we enjoy with other human beings on earth is also eternal.

The Resurrection of Jesus: At the very heart of the Christian faith is the belief that Jesus Christ rose from the dead. Christians see Jesus' resurrection as the prototype of all our 'resurrections'. As the apostle Paul put it: 'For as all die in Adam, even so all will be made alive in Christ' (1 Corinthians 15:22).

'The evidence for survival beyond death might one day present a challenge to Humanism as profound as that which Darwinian Evolution did to Christianity a century ago.'
DR JOHN BELOFF, WRITING IN *THE HUMANIST* MAGAZINE IN 1965.

Spring flowers among the gravestones of a churchyard are a reminder of the promise of life after death.

Views About Human Destiny

Extinction: We 'go out like a light' and cease to exist except in people's memories.

Immortality: A Greek idea, which profoundly influenced some Christian thinkers in the early centuries of the faith. This proposes that all human beings, having immortal 'souls', are therefore incapable of death.

Resuscitation: This belief, widely held in popular mythology, assumes that dead bodies are in some way brought back to life. It has led some people to be suspicious of organ donation or cremation, for instance.

Reincarnation: The belief of Buddhists and Hindus. This is the rebirth of a soul in a new body, either lower or higher on the ladder of existence. Souls that reach the top of the 'ladder' are caught up into the divine.

Resurrection: This is the belief of Christians. It sees the earthly human body as designed for life here and now, but proposes that God will 'clothe' the human spirit (the 'essence' of a person) in a new body suitable for life in the spiritual realm of heaven (1 Corinthians 15:35–56). The body of the risen Jesus as the disciples encountered him is seen as a model of this resurrection' body.

What People Have Said About Life After Death
••••••••••••••••••••

'I have good hope that there is something after death.'
PLATO

'We feel and know that we are eternal.'
BARUCH SPINOZA

'Death is the great adventure, beside which moon landings and space trips pale into insignificance.'
JOSEPH BAYLY

'The final heartbeat for the Christian is not the mysterious conclusion to a meaningless existence. It is, rather, the grand beginning to a life that will never end.'
JAMES DOBSON

'A belief in immortality has therapeutic power, because no one can live in peace in a house that he knows is shortly to tumble about his ears.'
CARL JUNG

'All we know of what they do above,
Is that they happy are, and that they love.'
EDMUND WALLER

The Resurrection, fresco (c.1444–50) by Andrea del Castagno at the Convent of St Apollonia, Florence, Italy.

A SUPERSTITIOUS AGE?

It is sometimes suggested that the idea of life after death was readily accepted in the early centuries of Christianity because that was a gullible or superstitious age. In fact the dominant school of Greek and Roman philosophy at the time was Stoicism, and one of the two most influential Jewish groups were the Sadducees. Both Stoics and Sadducees strongly rejected any notion of life after death.

MALCOLM MUGGERIDGE

'I often wake up in the night and feel myself in some curious way, half in and half out of my body… In that condition… two extraordinarily sharp impressions come to me. The first is of the incredible beauty of our earth – its colours and shapes, its smells and its features; of the enchantment of human love and companionship, and of the blessed fulfilment provided by human work and human procreation. And the second, a certainty surpassing all words and thoughts, that as an infinitesimal particle of God's creation, I am a participant in his purposes, which are loving and not malign, creative and not destructive, orderly and not chaotic, universal and not particular. And in that certainty, a great peace and a great joy.'

23

The Holy Spirit
GOD'S SPIRIT AT WORK IN THE WORLD

Christians see the Holy Spirit as the presence and power of God at work in people and in the world. The Spirit was present at the creation 'moving over the face of the waters' (Genesis 1:1). The Spirit of God inspires and guides many of the great figures in the history of Israel: Samuel, David, Elijah, Ezekiel and many more. In the New Testament the Holy Spirit was at work in the circumstances of the birth of John the Baptist (Luke 1:16, 41) and at the baptism of Jesus (Luke 3:22). On the Day of Pentecost the Holy Spirit 'fell' on the apostles, giving them both the courage and the words to speak to the crowds about the risen Jesus.

Christians believe that they are 'guided by the Spirit' (Galatians 5:25) and 'led by the Spirit' (Romans 8:14). It is the Holy Spirit who calls people to Christian ministry, and then enables them to do the things God has called them to do (Acts 13:2–4). Every Christian is said to possess the Spirit of Christ (Romans 8:9).

The Lord, the Giver of Life

In the Christian Creed the Holy Spirit is called 'the Lord, the giver of life'. In both the main languages of the Bible, Hebrew and Greek, the word for 'spirit' and the word for 'breath' are identical. What breathes, lives, and when we stop breathing, we die. So the Spirit of God is the divine 'breath', the essential difference between life and death. In the second Genesis story of the creation of man, God 'breathed into his nostrils the breath (spirit) of life' (Genesis 2:7). This relates to physical life, of course – God is its source, the Spirit is its agent. But there is also what Christians call 'spiritual' life, or 'eternal' life, and this too is brought about by the action of the Holy Spirit. The risen Jesus 'breathed' on his disciples to enable them to 'receive the Holy Spirit' (John 20:22), and at Pentecost the Holy Spirit came upon the assembled disciples as wind (again, the same word).

THE 'COMFORTER'

In older Bibles Jesus refers to the Holy Spirit as the 'Comforter' (see, for example, John 14:15), but that is only true in an archaic sense of the word (one who gives strength). Most modern translations refer to the Spirit as our 'Advocate' (one who is 'on our side'), 'Helper' or 'Counsellor' (source of wisdom and guidance). The actual word used in the New Testament is *parakletos*, which literally means something like 'helper alongside'. The Holy Spirit exists to help, strengthen, advise and stand alongside God's people.

The Day of Pentecost, when the Holy Spirit 'fell' on the disciples. From a twelfth-century Belgian lectionary.

24

● SEE ALSO
PENTECOST P88-89
THE EVANGELICALS P78-79

'TONGUES'

According to Acts chapter 2, on the Day of Pentecost the apostles were 'filled with the Spirit' and began to 'speak in other tongues' – preaching in languages that they did not previously know. This gift seems to have been present in the early days of the church, notably in the church at Corinth, though it is not clear whether the Christians there were able to speak in other languages, rather than a private 'language of the Spirit'. The apostle Paul gives guidance on the use of 'tongues', insisting that these utterances, if made in public, must be 'interpreted' (1 Corinthians 14:27, 28). All through the history of the church the gift seems to have been present from time to time, though there is some dispute as to whether these later instances are identical to the gift of tongues evident on the Day of Pentecost. In his first letter to the church at Corinth, Paul seems to imply that they aren't, in the sense that they are not intelligible to the hearers (see 1 Corinthians 14:13–19).

THE FRUIT OF THE SPIRIT

The Holy Spirit is said to produce in the lives of Christians the following qualities, known as the 'fruit of the Spirit' (Galatians 5:22).

Love

Joy

Peace

Patience

Kindness

Goodness

Faithfulness

Gentleness

Self-control

SEVEN GIFTS OF THE SPIRIT

See 1 Corinthians 12:7–11

Wisdom

Knowledge

Faith

Healing

Miracles

Prophecy

Tongues and the Interpretation of Tongues

John the Baptist baptizes Jesus, and the Holy Spirit descends on him in the form of a dove. Mural in Panormitis Monastery, Greece.

What the Spirit Does

Guides and Leads

If we live by the Spirit, let us also be guided by the Spirit.
GALATIANS 5:25

Teaches the Truth

When the Spirit of truth comes, he will guide you into all the truth.
JOHN 16:13

Draws People Closer to Jesus Christ

(The Holy Spirit) will glorify me, because he will take what is mine and declare it to you. All that the Father has is mine. For this reason I said that he will take what is mine and declare it to you.
JOHN 16:14, 15

Helps People to Pray

Likewise the Spirit helps us in our weakness; for we do not know how to pray as we ought, but that very Spirit intercedes with sighs too deep for words.
ROMANS 8:26

A JOYOUS MELODY

When Pope Gregory IV proclaimed Francis of Assisi to be a saint in 1228, and began to sing the *Te Deum*, 'there was raised a clamour among the many people praising God: the air was filled with their jubilations, and the ground was moistened with their tears. New songs were sung, and the servants of God jubilated in melody of the Spirit… a very sweet odour was breathed, and a most joyous melody that stirred the emotions resounded there.'
QUOTED BY JOHN GUNSTONE IN *PENTECOST COMES TO CHURCH*

Canonization from *Scenes from the Life of Saint Francis* by Giotto.

The Final Victory
'CHRIST WILL COME AGAIN'

It is an undisputed but also understated belief of Christians that Jesus, who lived on earth two thousand years ago, will one day return or 'come again'. That event will signal God's final victory over all that is evil and corrupt in his world, restoring it to the state in which he first created it. Jesus taught his disciples about this 'Second Coming' (often spoken of as the *parousia*, from the Greek word for 'appearing'), and the first Christians eagerly anticipated it. The Christian Creed simply says that 'he will come again in glory to judge the living and the dead, and his kingdom will have no end'.

The Second Coming underlines a deep truth: in the end, God's justice, love and peace will be supreme. The coming of this kingdom of God will be introduced by the appearing of his Son. Picture language is used in the Bible to describe this event, and from this many people have tried to describe what it will be like, and even when it will happen. However, Jesus said that it will take place at an unexpected time and in an unexpected form – just like his first coming, when he was born in a stable in Bethlehem.

This engraving from 1498 by Albrecht Durer is based on a vision described in the biblical book of Revelation. Here, God hands trumpets to seven angels to announce the end of the world.

What Jesus Said About His Second Coming

'Beware that no one leads you astray. Many will come in my name and say, "I am he!" and they will lead many astray. When you hear of wars and rumours of wars, do not be alarmed; this must take place, but the end is still to come.'
MARK 13:5–7

'But about that day or hour no one knows, neither the angels in heaven, nor the Son, but only the Father. Beware, keep alert; for you do not know when the time will come.'
MARK 13:32, 33

Once Jesus was asked by the Pharisees when the kingdom of God was coming, and he answered, 'The kingdom of God is not coming with things that can be observed; nor will they say, "Look, here it is!" or "There it is!" For, in fact, the kingdom of God is among you.'
LUKE 17:20, 21

'They will say to you, "Look there!" or "Look here!" Do not go, do not set off in pursuit.For as the lightning flashes and lights up the sky from one side to the other, so will the Son of Man be in his day.'
LUKE 17:23, 24

'Then the sign of the Son of Man will appear in heaven, and then all the tribes of the earth will mourn, and they will see "the Son of Man coming on the clouds of heaven" with power and great glory. And he will send out his angels with a loud trumpet call, and they will gather his elect from the four winds, from one end of heaven to the other.'
MATTHEW 24:30, 31

DANIEL'S VISION

The prophet Daniel, whose visions of the future are recorded in the book bearing his name, lived in the sixth century BCE. Jesus picked up one of those visions and applied it to himself:

As I watched in the night visions, I saw one like a human being (literally, one like a son of man) coming with the clouds of heaven. And he came to the Ancient One and was presented before him.
DANIEL 7:13

THE FORECASTERS

Over the centuries there have been many people, groups and sects, within and on the fringes of Christianity, who have foretold with great confidence the date of Christ's Second Coming. At the end of the first millennium many people were convinced that the 'thousand years' spoken of in the New Testament had been fulfilled and Jesus would return (see Revelation 20:7). Needless to say, up to now all forecasters have been wrong.

REVELATION

The book of Revelation, the last in the Bible, offers a series of visions of the final victory of God and 'the Lamb' (Christ) over the powers of evil and darkness. In colourful and at times gory language it depicts the last stand of God's enemies and their eventual downfall. The final chapters reveal a very different picture – the 'new heaven and new earth' where there is no longer any pain, sorrow, bereavement or tears, and where people live in harmony and joy in a golden city (Revelation 21 and 22). The visions end with the promise of Jesus that he will 'come quickly' and the cry of the believers, 'Amen. Come, Lord Jesus!'

MARTIN LUTHER

The great leader of the Reformation in Europe in the fifteenth century, Martin Luther, wrote this about the Second Coming of Jesus:

'Christ designed that the day of his coming should be hid from us, so that, being in suspense, we might be, as it were, upon the watch.'

This mural by Giotto of the Last Judgment covers the entire wall of the Scrovegni Chapel in Padua, Italy.

The Ladder of Virtue and the Last Judgement, a sixteenth-century fresco at Sucevita Monastery, Moldavia, Romania.

Disciples
'FOLLOWING WITH PURPOSE'

The first followers of Jesus were called, as we have seen, his 'disciples', and the word has stuck. Those who follow Jesus are still his 'disciples' and the process of following him is called 'discipleship'. The root of the word is from Latin – 'to learn'. A disciple is a 'learner', which by extension is a follower. The disciples of Jesus sit at his feet, as it were, to be taught by him, and follow his lead, to be guided by him. Every Christian is therefore a permanent learner.

The process of learning or following is life-long, which should evoke a certain modesty or reticence on the part of Christians where absolute 'knowledge' is concerned. In every way, the believer seeks to follow Jesus. All the time, the believer learns more and more about what it means to be his disciple. Baptism, in other words, is not a 'passing-out parade', but the first step on a long journey of faith. The Christian's journey is not meant to be an aimless ramble, but a pilgrimage with purpose – travelling in search of light and truth, led all the way by a Master who claimed to be both the light of the world and the truth of God.

An Iranian shepherd leading his sheep.

What Jesus Said About Following Him

And Jesus said to them, 'Follow me, and I will make you fish for people.'
MATTHEW 4:19

Then Jesus said to them all, 'If any want to become my followers, let them deny themselves and take up their cross daily and follow me.'
LUKE 9:23

'Whoever serves me must follow me, and where I am, there will my servant be also.'
JOHN 12:26

'My sheep hear my voice. I know them, and they follow me.'
JOHN 10:27

The Reluctant Followers

As they were going along the road, someone said to him, 'I will follow you wherever you go.' And Jesus said to him, 'Foxes have holes, and birds of the air have nests; but the Son of Man has nowhere to lay his head.'
To another he said, 'Follow me.' But he said, 'Lord, first let me go and bury my father.' But Jesus said to him, 'Let the dead bury their own dead; but as for you, go and proclaim the kingdom of God.'
Another said, 'I will follow you, Lord; but let me first say farewell to those at my home.' Jesus said to him, 'No one who puts a hand to the plough and looks back is fit for the kingdom of God.'
LUKE 9:57–62

The ploughman keeps his eyes constantly looking ahead. Once he turns round, he starts to plough a crooked furrow.

The Life of the Disciple

The life of the follower of Jesus involves at least four basic elements:

Faith: Faith is trust, and there is no point in following a guide we do not trust.

Prayer: Prayer is a two-way conversation in which the follower communicates with the leader, and the leader communicates with the follower.

Belonging: The follower of Jesus becomes by right and responsibility a member of the whole community of his followers – that's to say, the Christian church. The journey is not a solo one, but is made in the company of others.

Service: Those who follow Jesus 'serve' him, and serve others. There are no 'non-playing' members.

The trust placed by a mountaineer in his guide could prove critical.

'Making Disciples'

Jesus called his followers to 'make disciples', which seems to involve rather more than simply making 'converts'. He wanted the people who were already learning from him and following him to find others who would learn in the same way and follow on the same path. As can be seen in what is called his 'Great Commission', given after his resurrection, making disciples involved baptizing (bringing people into the community of faith) and teaching. It also involved a promise: that he would stay with them 'all the road' (the literal meaning of the word 'always' which he used).

And Jesus came and said to them, 'All authority in heaven and on earth has been given to me. Go therefore and make disciples of all nations, baptizing them in the name of the Father and of the Son and of the Holy Spirit, and teaching them to obey everything that I have commanded you. And remember, I am with you always, to the end of the age.'
MATTHEW 28:18–20

WILLIAM PENN: THE TRUE DISCIPLE

'The way of God is a way of faith, as dark to sense as mortal to self. It is the children of obedience, "who count", with holy Paul, "all things dross that they may win Christ", who know and walk in this narrow way. Speculation will not do, nor can refined motions enter; the obedient only eat the good of this land. "They who do his will", says the blessed Jesus, "shall know of my doctrine; them he will instruct."'

William Penn, an English Quaker, sailed to the New World in 1682 to flee religious persecution. He founded the State of Pennsylvania, USA.

Monks in procession at Bec Abbey in France.

Meeting Needs
WHO IS MY NEIGHBOUR?

Most people probably know that the Bible tells us to 'love our neighbours'. In modern language that usually means the people who live next door or very near us – 'Have you got nice neighbours?' is a common question. However, the Bible extends the notion of 'neighbourliness' beyond that. In the Hebrew Scriptures your 'neighbour' might be anyone who lives or works nearby, a friend or partner, or simply a fellow-Israelite. Jesus took the concept even further: my 'neighbour' is the person who needs my help, whatever his or her race and wherever they happen to live.

Because of this commandment to 'love your neighbour', Christians have never been able to live as though other people didn't exist. My neighbour is the one who needs me and the one to whom I should offer love. This principle has driven Christians and churches to explore ways of being 'good neighbours', serving individuals and the community without looking for any payback themselves. The commandment has no escape clauses or conditions attached to it: to 'love' is to serve.

Commandments About 'Neighbours'

You shall not take vengeance or bear a grudge against any of your people, but you shall love your neighbour as yourself.
LEVITICUS 19:18

You shall not bear false witness against your neighbour.
EXODUS 20:16

You shall not covet your neighbour's house; you shall not covet your neighbour's wife; or male or female slave, or ox, or donkey, or anything that belongs to your neighbour.
EXODUS 20:17

Love does no wrong to a neighbour, therefore love is the fulfilling of the law.
ROMANS 13:10

The Good Samaritan

In this well-known story, Jesus demonstrated that the test of neighbourliness is not racial identity or simply living near someone, but an attitude of mind. A Jewish man was set upon by robbers on the road from Jerusalem to Jericho, beaten, robbed and left at the roadside half dead. Two devout religious figures came along the road, a priest and a Levite (a Temple servant). Both saw the man lying there, but 'passed by on the other side'. Then a Samaritan, a member of a race despised by the Jews for their religious practices, came by. He saw the man, took pity on him, treated his wounds, put him on his donkey and took him to an inn, where he paid the bill for him to stay there until he had recovered. 'Which one was neighbour to the man who fell among thieves?' Jesus asked – and got the correct answer, 'The one who showed him mercy' (Luke 10:25–37).

Homeless young people on a London street. The same scene is re-enacted in cities all over the world.

THE TRUE NEIGHBOUR

Father Damien was a member of the Order of Fathers of the Sacred Heart of Jesus and Mary. In 1863 he was sent by his Order to the Hawaiian islands as a missionary. At his own request, he went to live in a leper settlement at Molokai, even though he knew that by doing so he risked contracting the deadly disease. He ministered single-handedly to the spiritual and physical needs of the 600 lepers who lived there. Eventually he too contracted leprosy, and felt that at last he was truly identified with the people to whom he ministered. He died of the disease in 1889.

Father Damien

How Do Christians 'Love Their Neighbours'?

■ By works of mercy – founding and staffing hospitals, hospices, orphanages, and so on.

■ By being honest and generous in speaking of others.

■ By avoiding envy and enjoying the success of others.

■ By individual acts of kindness and thoughtfulness.

A boy at the Bulgiri School for the Blind in Dodoma, Tanzania. A comprehensive education is given to blind children from surrounding villages. The school belongs to the Church of England, but receives funding from different Christian charities.

What People Have Said About Neighbours

'*The correlative to loving our neighbours as ourselves is hating ourselves as we hate our neighbours.*'
OLIVER WENDELL HOLMES SR

'*The good neighbour looks beyond the external accidents and discerns those inner qualities that make all men human and therefore brothers.*'
MARTIN LUTHER KING

'*Mix with the neighbours and you learn what's doing in your own house.*'
YIDDISH PROVERB

'*Help your brother's boat across, and your own will reach the shore.*'
HINDU PROVERB

'*Every man's neighbour is his looking glass.*'
ENGLISH PROVERB

The preparation of food supplements is demonstrated to a group of mothers in a village in Mozambique. The project is run by World Vision, an international Christian relief organisation.

'AS YOURSELF'

This intriguing phrase presumably means that our love for our 'neighbour' should equal our love for ourselves. This of course implies that we are able to love ourselves, which some people find quite difficult. The plain meaning of the words is that we should value the life, well-being and happiness of our 'neighbour' as much as we value our own.

Mother Teresa in her home for the destitute and dying in Calcutta. 'When I see these people, I see Jesus,' she once said.

Grace
THE UNDESERVED GIFT

'Grace' is a word that keeps cropping up in connection with Christianity. It's the subject of many books and sermons and the theme of many hymns. The Reformation was fought, very largely, over the way Christians should understand the role of 'grace' in the relationship of human beings to God. Whatever it is, it's clearly important.

That 'whatever' is the problem! Grace lies at the heart of the Christian understanding of God, but it's not always a simple concept to describe. At its root grace means an unearned or undeserved gift, and from the beginning of the Bible those closest to God have recognized that all that they have, whether material or spiritual, comes to them as such a gift. We haven't 'earned' the right even to exist; it is a gift. But so are daily life, human love and God's forgiveness.

The best example of grace, for Christians, is the life of Jesus. 'God so loved the world that he gave his only Son' (John 3:16). Jesus so loved the world that he gave his own life for us. That is why it is by grace, as the apostle Paul argues, that we have been 'saved through faith'. Even our very faith is not our own doing, he says: 'it is the gift of God' (Ephesians 2:8).

In everyday language, 'grace' means 'elegance of movement', 'courtesy', 'attractiveness'. But the Bible has a special meaning for it: the free and unearned favour of God.

In the Old Testament

'Grace' is understood as God's 'favour' or 'kindness' in the Old Testament, mostly in the way he blesses and protects Israel. Underlying their whole image of God, however, the Jewish people saw him as the source and giver of everything, from existence itself to the provision of daily food and water (Psalm 34:10).

In the New Testament

'Grace' is frequently used by the apostle Paul to describe the sacrificial love of Christ:

For you know the grace of our Lord Jesus Christ, that though he was rich, yet for your sakes he became poor, so that by his poverty you might become rich.
2 CORINTHIANS 8:9

Grace is a free gift of God, simply to be received with open hands and a grateful heart.

What People Have Said About Grace

'A state of mind that sees God in everything is evidence of growth in grace and a thankful heart.'
CHARLES G. FINNEY

'Grace is not sought, nor bought, nor wrought. It is a free gift of Almighty God to needy mankind.'
BILLY GRAHAM

'They travel lightly whom God's grace carries.'
THOMAS À KEMPIS

'Grace grows best in the winter.'
SAMUEL RUTHERFORD

'Grace does not destroy nature, it perfects it.'
THOMAS AQUINAS

JOHN NEWTON

John Newton (1725–1807) was the captain of a slave-trader ship, transporting slaves from West Africa to the Americas. Following a Christian conversion, he eventually became an ardent opponent of the slave trade, a supporter of William Wilberforce's efforts to get a bill through the British parliament to abolish it, and a gifted writer of hymns. While he was rector of Olney, in Buckinghamshire, he wrote the hymn 'Amazing grace', which has been translated into many languages all over the world, and which is largely his own story. It includes this verse:

*Through many dangers, toils and snares
I have already come.
'Tis grace that brought me safe thus far,
And grace will lead me home.*

THE GIFT OF GOD

Every religion starts from the same position: 'God' is good, and we are not. That's the problem. Each then offers its own distinctive answer to the problem. Most require the seeker to do or be something special to come to God: observe the Five Pillars of Islam; obey the Torah (the Law); meditate and reflect to lift ourselves up into the divine. Of the great world faiths only Christianity asks nothing of its disciples except to come with open hands and open hearts to receive the gift of God. If religion is supremely a ladder from where we are to where God is, then the Christian case is the odd one out, because it claims that God came 'down' to us, in Jesus, to lift us from where we are and bring us to himself. That is grace.

Not your own doing

For by grace you have been saved through faith, and this is not your own doing; it is the gift of God – not the result of works, so that no one may boast.
EPHESIANS 2:8

Uniquely among religions, Christianity teaches that it is not possible to do or achieve anything in order to be acceptable to God. Instead, he took the initiative and came down as Jesus to reach us.

Good things about grace

1. It stops the believer boasting.

2. It reminds believers that God is a God of love.

3. It creates faith, hope and love in response to God's generosity.

4. Those who have received grace should show it to others.

5. All are equal. Grace has no favourites.

Problems with grace

1. It could give the impression that faith and action are in themselves pointless. In fact, faith is the channel by which we receive grace, and our actions ('works', in Bible language) are the evidence of its presence in our lives.

2. People could presume on God's generosity by taking it for granted, rather than allowing it to change their lives.

3. Some might imagine that if God is so generous then he won't mind how they behave.

4. Others might believe that the gift of God's grace isn't for everyone, but only for a chosen few.

5. Because God's gift is free, people might be suspicious of it – 'there's no such thing as a free lunch'.

Worship
THE 'LOVE FEAST'

'Worship' comes naturally to human beings, both individually and collectively. Think of the besotted young man gazing into the eyes of his beloved and saying, in all sincerity, 'You are so beautiful, darling!' Or, for contrast, think of a crowd of football fans, wearing their replica shirts, and chanting the name of their team over and over again. Those are examples of worship – irrational at one level, extravagant, impulsive and at that moment all-consuming.

Seen in those terms, it isn't surprising that Christians should also offer worship to God, sometimes on their own, in prayer or reflection, and sometimes collectively, as they gather in church. At its most authentic, worship for Christians would also be impulsive, all-consuming, extravagant and beyond cool reason. After all, God is the source of their life. His kingdom is their goal. His will is the means by which they hope to reach it. And it is through his love, shown to them in Jesus Christ, that Christians have been drawn to faith in him. There is really nothing 'odd' about worship!

WORSHIP IS 'NATURAL'

'It is a law of human nature, written into our very essence, and just as much a part of us as the desire to build houses and cultivate the land and marry and have children and read books and sing songs, that we should want to stand together with others in order to acknowledge our common dependence on God, our Father and our Creator.'

THOMAS MERTON, TRAPPIST MONK OF THE ABBEY OF OUR LADY OF GETHSEMANE, KENTUCKY, USA

How the First Christians Did It

In the book of Acts Luke gives us a picture of the worship of the first Christians – the 120 or so who had gathered in the Upper Room after the resurrection and the 3,000 that he reports were baptized on the Day of Pentecost. They continued, he says, 'in the apostles' teaching and fellowship, in the breaking of bread and the prayers' (Acts 2:42). He then expands this to give us a picture of a community that shared its possessions, its meals and its affection, meeting in each other's homes and eating their food 'with glad and generous hearts'. They 'broke bread' from house to house, praising God and having 'the goodwill of all the people'.

The apostle Paul, 20 or so years later, describes the worship of the church at Corinth in Greece, where it seems they gathered for a common meal (the 'love feast') and then shared Holy Communion (see 1 Corinthians 11:17–28). This would have been on the 'first day of the week' (Sunday), but as it was a normal working day they must have met either at dawn, before work, or in the evening.

A Greek pilgrim prays in the grotto in Jerusalem where it is reputed that Jesus was imprisoned before his crucifixion.

Worship Today

The 'normal' day for Christians to gather for worship is still the first day of the week, Sunday. They chose this day because it was the day of Christ's resurrection. In many countries today people work on a Sunday, and increasingly Saturday evenings or weekdays are also used for worship. Whichever day of the week it takes place, Christian worship invariably includes the reading of the Bible, prayer and praise (usually in song).

Many Christian churches regularly join in the 'breaking of bread' (Holy Communion or Eucharist), and there will also often be a 'Service of the Word' (based around teaching and studying the Bible). 'Informal worship' – including songs and hymns and spontaneous prayer – is also part of the regular pattern in many churches.

● SEE ALSO
BREAD AND WINE P92-93
HYMNS AND SONGS P98-99
SOLEMN SONGS P96-97

A Palestinian Christian reaches out towards an icon of the Virgin Mary during a visit to the Church of the Nativity in Bethlehem.

What People Have Said About Worship

'The man who has learned to love a new life has learned to sing a new song. For a new man, a new song and the New Testament all belong to the same kingdom.'
AUGUSTINE OF HIPPO

'A little lifting of the heart suffices; a little remembrance of God; one act of inward worship – these are prayers which, however short, are nevertheless acceptable to God.'
BROTHER LAWRENCE

'A man can no more diminish God's glory by refusing to worship him than a lunatic can put out the sun by scribbling the word "darkness" on the walls of his cell.'
C. S. LEWIS

'Worship is not a part of the Christian life; it is the Christian life.'
GERALD VANN

'The Bible begins with creation and ends with worship. That is the direction in which we must all move… The purpose and peace of mankind is to be found in the worship of the one who created us.'
BISHOP MICHAEL MARSHALL

ADORATION

'To worship is to quicken the conscience by the holiness of God, to feed the mind with the truth of God, to purge the imagination by the beauty of God, to open the heart to the love of God, to devote the will to the purpose of God. All this is gathered up in that emotion which most cleanses us from selfishness because it is the most selfless of all emotions – adoration.'
ARCHBISHOP WILLIAM TEMPLE

An open-air mass being celebrated at the Jasna Gora Monastery in Czestochowa, Poland.

Prayer
LIFELINE TO THE UNSEEN GOD

It's often said that everyone prays sometimes, even if it's only when the pilot says all the engines have failed. Actually it's quite puzzling that the practice of talking to a Power or Person we can't see in the hope that they can make our situation better has such widespread support, especially when many of those who pray would admit that they're not sure whether God exists. As far as we can go back in human history, it seems, people have prayed, and in our modern scientific and technological age millions upon millions of people still do.

Prayer lies at the heart of Christianity, as it does in the Judaism from which it grew. Jesus himself prayed and taught his followers to pray. Even as he was dying on the cross, he prayed. We know from the book of Acts that the first Christians prayed constantly and we can read many of the prayers of the great apostle Paul in his letters. Sometimes those early Christians were asking God to do something. Sometimes they were seeking guidance. Sometimes they were simply thanking him for something he had done. Prayer encompasses all of those elements and, as we shall see, several more as well.

Questions About Prayer

1. Isn't prayer really a matter of trying to get God to change his mind?

2. If God is good and all-powerful, as Christians say, why doesn't he just do good things without any need for us to ask him?

3. Surely prayer can't change 'things' – the weather, for instance, or a fatal illness, or whether the public address system works properly?

4. Isn't prayer really a refuge for people who can't manage life as it is and want to call up some unseen power to intervene on their behalf?

Answers to Questions

1. If prayer were a matter of trying to get God to change his mind it would be futile! Prayer is a collaboration with God in the fulfilling of his will: he gives us the privilege of sharing in what he is doing.

2. At the same time, part of God's will for us is that we should learn to ask, and find our relationship with him deepened and strengthened when he answers our prayers. So it would seem that sometimes he waits until we ask, so that when that prayer is answered, faith will be reinforced.

3. Generally Christian prayer is not about changing 'things', but people – and prayer has proved very effective at that! If people change, very often things change too.

4. There can't be many people who haven't at some time or other felt that things had got beyond them, and yes, to turn to God for help in such circumstances seems very sensible. However, just as a telephone can be used for many purposes beyond making emergency calls, it's a caricature of prayer simply to use it in moments of desperate need.

Catholic Christians at prayer in a remote village in China.

ESSENTIAL ELEMENTS OF PRAYER

In the Christian tradition prayer normally includes these essential elements:

Repentance: Admitting our faults to God and seeking forgiveness.

Requests (petition): Bringing to God our own needs and those of others.

Reflection: on some aspect of God's character, love or work.

Thanksgiving: for past mercies, answered prayers and daily blessings.

Prayer in Church

Many churches use a formal 'liturgy' (a set pattern of worship) for public services. The priest or minister leads and the congregation joins in with 'responses'. In the last 50 years it has been the practice in most churches that employ a liturgy to include in the service a time when one or more members lead the congregation in prayer. This may follow a set form or be spontaneous.

Other churches do not use a set liturgy, but construct public worship around the elements of singing, preaching and praying. The Bible will be read and the Lord's Supper may be shared.

From early times the 'Great Prayer' of the church has been the 'Eucharistic Thanksgiving', the prayer in which the one presiding gives thanks for the bread and wine and repeats the 'words of institution' first spoken by Jesus on the night of his betrayal.

The congregation at prayer during an evangelical church service in Armenia.

The Lord's Prayer recognizes our daily need for food.

'PRIVATE' PRAYER

Prayer is an essential part of the life of a Christian. Part of this 'prayer life' may be experienced with others, whether in large congregations or small groups. However, many Christians also make

time to pray on their own – setting aside a certain time each day to read part of the Bible and then pray, probably silently. Those prayers will include petitions (requests), but also usually involve the other essential elements of prayer.

The Lord's Prayer

The disciples of Jesus asked him to teach them to pray, and he gave them this 'pattern prayer', which we know as the Lord's Prayer:

Our Father in heaven,
hallowed be your name;
your kingdom come, your will be done,
on earth as in heaven.
Give us this day our daily bread,
and forgive us our sins,
as we forgive those who sin against us.
Lead us not into temptation, but deliver us from evil.
For the kingdom, the power and the glory are yours,
now and for ever. Amen.

What People Have Said About Prayer

'Prayer is not an old woman's idle amusement. Properly understood and applied, it is the most potent instrument of action.'
MAHATMA GHANDI

'Prayer is the contemplation of the facts of life from the highest point of view.'
RALPH WALDO EMERSON

'None can pray well but he that lives well.'
THOMAS FULLER

'Prayer is conversation with God.'
CLEMENT OF ALEXANDRIA

'Pray to God, but continue to row to the shore.'
RUSSIAN PROVERB

'The purpose of all prayer is to find God's will and to make that will our prayer.'
CATHERINE MARSHALL

'What's important is that God is so much part and parcel of life that spontaneous mental chat becomes second nature.'
CLIFF RICHARD

Miyacles
ACTIONS THAT SPEAK LOUDER THAN WORDS?

Christians believe in miracles. Well, they certainly believe in one, because the absolute foundation of their faith is that Jesus Christ was raised from the dead. Miracles don't come much bigger than that.

According to the dictionary, a miracle is 'an extraordinary and welcome event attributed to a divine agency'. By that definition, there are many miracles in the Bible, from the crossing of the Red Sea by the Israelites to the water that Jesus changed into wine in John's Gospel.

In fact, Christians don't believe in miracles as such, but in God. As he brought into being the entire universe, light and life itself, it isn't difficult to see why Jesus said that 'what is impossible for mortals is possible for God' (Luke 18:27). In the context of the greatest of all miracles, the existence of the universe itself and of life within it, most of the biblical miracles seem quite modest.

That doesn't mean that everything that the biblical writers saw as a 'miracle' was necessarily a supernatural event. See, for instance, the story of the crossing of the Red Sea, and notice how a perfectly rational explanation is given for the actual event (Exodus 14:21). The 'miracle' was in the timing!

MIRACLES OR 'SIGNS'?

John's Gospel records seven 'miracles' of Jesus, but never calls them that. The writer very carefully describes them as 'signs', and a sign, of course, points away from itself to something else. The miracles in the Gospels are like that: we are not invited to get involved in the 'nuts and bolts' of how they happened, but to see the thing to which they are pointing – usually, an insight into the nature, power and love of Jesus.

What People Have Said About Miracles

'There is in every miracle a silent chiding of the world, and a tacit reprehension of them who require, or need miracles.'
JOHN DONNE, POET AND DEAN OF ST PAUL'S, LONDON

'Miracles enable us to judge of doctrine, and doctrine enables us to judge of miracles.'
BLAISE PASCAL, PENSÉES

'The supernatural is the natural not yet understood.'
ELBERT HUBBARD, THE NOTE BOOK

'There are more things in heaven and earth, Horatio, than are dreamt of in your philosophy.'
SHAKESPEARE, HAMLET

Types of Miracle

Healing: The most common miracles performed by Jesus were those which involved healing of individuals, physically, mentally or spiritually.

Feeding or providing: Examples include the provision of manna in the desert for the Israelites (Exodus 16:14–16) and Jesus feeding 5,000 people with five loaves and two small fishes (Mark 6:30–44).

Rescuing: For example, Daniel in the lions' den (Daniel 6:16–23) and the release of the apostle Peter from prison (Acts 12:6–11).

Christ feeds the 5000. A mosaic from the Chora Church, Istanbul, Turkey.

Ten Biblical Miracles

1. The burning bush: Moses saw a bush that was burning but wasn't being consumed. He drew near, and God spoke to him (Exodus 3:1–6).

2. Daniel in the lions' den: Daniel was thrown into a den of lions as punishment for disobeying an edict of the king of Babylon. In the morning he was found alive and well (Daniel 6:19–22).

3. Water into wine: At a wedding in Cana, whenthe wine ran out, Jesus turned 150 gallons (682 litres) of water into wine for the guests (John 2:1–11).

4. The paralytic: Jesus healed a paralysed man who was lowered through the roof of the house where Jesus was by four friends (Mark 2:3–12).

5. The ten lepers: Jesus healed ten people suffering from leprosy, but only one, a despised Samaritan, came back to thank God (Luke 17:11–19).

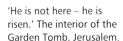

Jesus Opens the Eyes of a Man Born Blind from the *Maesta* Altarpiece by Duccio di Buoninsegna.

6. The woman with an issue of blood: Jesus healed a woman who for 12 years had suffered from persistent bleeding (Luke 8:43–48).

7. Blind Bartimaeus: A beggar at the gates of Jericho had his sight restored by Jesus (Mark 10:46–52).

8. The raising of Lazarus: Jesus brought his friend Lazarus back from the dead four days after he had been buried (John 11:38–43).

9. The man lame from birth: The apostles Peter and John healed a lame man at the gate of the Temple (Acts 3:2–8).

10. Dorcas: Peter raised a woman called Dorcas, a member of the church in Joppa, from the dead (Acts 9:36–38).

Jesus raising Lazarus after four days in the tomb. From an Armenian Evangelistery dated around 1280.

'He is not here – he is risen.' The interior of the Garden Tomb, Jerusalem.

THE GREATEST MIRACLE

Undoubtedly, the greatest miracle in the Bible, other than the creation itself, is the resurrection of Jesus. After his death by crucifixion his body was laid in a tomb cut in the rock face of a garden nearby. A round stone was rolled into position to close the entrance to the tomb. On the Sunday – the 'third day' after his crucifixion – women came to anoint his body but found the tomb empty and the body gone. They were told that Jesus was 'not there' – he had risen. And so they and others discovered as he appeared to them over the following days.

Self-Denial

ABSTINENCE - A WAY OF LIFE?

Every religion urges its followers to practise abstinence – to deny themselves things or activities that would hinder their relationship with God. Christianity is no exception, though generally speaking it has not made such abstinence a matter of strict rules, but of personal choice.

There were fasts as well as feasts in the Jewish religion in Bible times. Jesus ridiculed those who ostentatiously advertised the fact that they were fasting by daubing ashes on their faces. During the Feast of Passover, however, all observant Jews abstained (and still do) from eating anything with yeast in it, and we may assume Jesus and his disciples also followed this practice. In the early days of the church, Christians continued to use fasting (denying oneself food) on special occasions or for particular purposes. The Christians at Antioch, for instance, were 'praying and fasting' when 'the Holy Spirit said, "Separate Saul (Paul) and Barnabas for the work to which I have called them"'(Acts 13:2). Fasting became a feature of the spiritual discipline of the Desert Fathers in the fourth century and was a key element in the life of monks and nuns from then on.

Jesus and Fasting

Jesus fasted in the desert after his baptism, and was put to the test by Satan (Matthew 4:1–11).

Disciples of Jesus were to 'deny themselves' and 'take up the cross' and follow him (Mark 9:34).

While the disciples of John the Baptist fasted, the disciples of Jesus didn't – and in everyday life, neither did he (Luke 7:33, 34).

He told his followers that when they were fasting they should not look 'dismal', but act in a normal way, observing their fast 'secretly' (Matthew 6:16–18).

The ultimate in asceticism? Saint Symeon Stylites, a fifth-century Syrian, spent 30 years on top of a 72-foot (22-metre) pillar preaching to the crowds. He is shown here on a sixteenth-century tempera and gold panel from Russia.

Temptation of Christ on the Mountain from the Maesta Altarpiece by Duccio di Buoninsegna.

An Ethiopian Orthodox monk living in a hole in red volcanic rock near the church in Lalibela, Ethiopia.

'BODILY AUSTERITIES'

'We will not, of course, rule out for ourselves, or for others, the practice, or at least the spirit, of bodily austerities. The spirit, and even some mild amount of the actual practice of such austerities is an integral constituent of all virile religion. The man who laughs at the plank bed and the discipline is a shallow fool.'

BARON FRIEDRICH VON HUEGEL

Seasons of Fasting

From early times the church has observed the 42 days of Lent as a fast, though Sundays are exempt. Generally speaking, the Lenten fast has not meant eating no food at all, but eating modestly and less frequently. The fast has been observed more rigorously in the Orthodox Churches than elsewhere; the Roman Catholic Church relaxed its rules on fasting at the Second Vatican Council of 1965.

Traditionally, Fridays (the day of the crucifixion of Jesus) have also been times of fasting in the Catholic Church. Until recent times this involved abstinence from meat, which accounts for the 'fish on Friday' tradition.

In the Orthodox Churches there are no fewer than 120 days stipulated as days of fasting in the year.

Christians in other churches also practise abstinence, of course, including fasting (particularly during special times of prayer) and Lent. The Salvation Army started the practice of 'self-denial weeks' as a means of raising money for the poor. Today that often expresses itself in church 'Lent Lunches', when a frugal meal is eaten but the price of a normal one is donated to charity.

LIVES OF ABSTINENCE

Ascetics: People who deny themselves the pleasures of the senses by abstinence from food, sex, human company and creature comforts.

Hermits: Those who have taken a vow to live in isolation from the world and its temptations.

Monks and Nuns: Those who have taken vows of poverty, chastity and obedience to the Rule of their Order.

THE OBJECTIVES OF CHRISTIAN ABSTINENCE

■ To exercise control over the body and its desires – what the apostle Paul called 'enslaving the body' (1 Corinthians 9:27).

■ To counter a concern with possessions.

■ To seek the 'treasure' of a spiritual life (Matthew 6:19–21).

■ To master sin and not be its slave (Romans 6:16).

THE DANGERS OF CHRISTIAN ABSTINENCE

■ Spiritual pride.

■ Devaluing God's gifts of human company and sexual love.

■ What the apostle Paul called 'will-worship'.

■ Regarding the physical body as evil, leading to self-harm, flagellation and the like.

The Monasteries
POVERTY, CHASTITY, OBEDIENCE

Modern people often say that they'd like to 'get away from it all', by which they usually mean spending a lazy couple of weeks on a beach in the Caribbean. But from the early days of the church there have been Christians who have taken the idea much more literally. They have sought to renounce the 'world' – its values, lifestyle and choices – and live a life dedicated to poverty, chastity and obedience: as you might say, no money, no sex and no independence.

Christians who have felt called to this kind of life came to be known as monks (men) and nuns (women). Some of them lived as hermits, in almost total isolation from company of any kind. Others – eventually, the majority – lived in communities, where they were able to follow a pattern of worship, prayer, reading and work. Monks and nuns take solemn and life-long vows (though in modern times it has become possible for them to be released from these). The members of the Order submit to the authority of the head of the community – prior, abbot or mother superior – and are left with few choices of their own to make.

How it Began

In the early church there was a strong element of asceticism (avoiding sensory pleasures or luxuries), which by the fourth century began to find expression in the lives of Christians known as the 'Desert Fathers'. The best-known of them was St Antony of Egypt, who lived the life of a hermit in the deserts near the Red Sea. A community of his followers adopted a similar lifestyle; but at the same time others, some of them following the example of St Pachomius, adopted a similarly disciplined way of life but lived in community.

The Temptation of Saint Anthony of Egypt by Domenico Morelli.

THE DAILY 'OFFICE'

Daily prayer and worship in monasteries and convents follows a set pattern, but different Orders and communities vary it to meet local circumstances. Today, the Daily Office, even if in a simplified form, is still the basis of the devotional life of a monastic community.

In each part of the office there will be Scripture readings, readings from other books in the monastic tradition, and the singing of psalms.

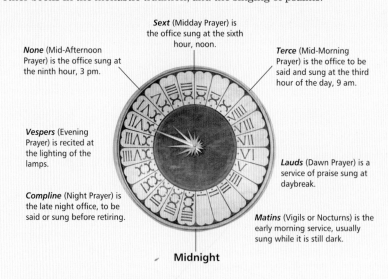

Sext (Midday Prayer) is the office sung at the sixth hour, noon.

Terce (Mid-Morning Prayer) is the office to be said and sung at the third hour of the day, 9 am.

None (Mid-Afternoon Prayer) is the office sung at the ninth hour, 3 pm.

Vespers (Evening Prayer) is recited at the lighting of the lamps.

Lauds (Dawn Prayer) is a service of praise sung at daybreak.

Compline (Night Prayer) is the late night office, to be said or sung before retiring.

Matins (Vigils or Nocturns) is the early morning service, usually sung while it is still dark.

Midnight

The fifteenth-century clock on the cathedral at Florence indicating the times of the prayers of the Daily Office. This style of 24-hour clock was used until the eighteenth century.

● SEE ALSO
HEROES AND MARTYRS OF THE PAST P42
PRAYER P36-37
SELF-DENIAL P40-41

Prayer and Work

The life of a typical convent or monastery is a combination of prayer, worship and work. The work may take various forms. Some enclosed Orders regard their life of prayer as 'work' – *orare est labore*, 'to pray is to work' – but in most cases there is specific labour, either manual or intellectual, to be done. Many nuns, for instance, teach in schools or nurse in hospitals and hospices. Monks teach in theological institutions or schools. At the more practical level, monasteries and convents have been renowned for producing and selling wine, cheese, incense, pottery and artwork. Others have extensive land, which is farmed.

The daily work takes place in between the allotted hours of prayer, though sometimes, in the interests of efficiency, the monks are permitted to say their prayers out in the fields.

A nun accompanies girls on their way to school at a convent and orphanage at Georgetown, Guyana.

DISTINGUISHED MONKS AND NUNS

Benedict (480–550 CE), known as the 'Patriarch of Western Monasticism', even though it seems he never intended to found an Order himself. The Rule of Benedict, which he drew up for his community at Monte Casino, has become the pattern for most monastic rules of life since.

Hildegard of Bingen (1098–1179), abbess of Rupertsberg, was a mystic who recorded her visions in a number of books. She also composed dramatic songs of astonishing originality and power.

Francis of Assisi (1181–1226), patron saint of Italy and founder of the Franciscan Order, was devoted to a simple and sacrificial lifestyle. His concern for the unity under God of the whole creation has made him popular with modern environmentalists.

Julian of Norwich (1342–1416), English mystic and spiritual writer, was an 'anchoress' (recluse) who spent much of her life in a single 'cell' attached to St Julian's Church in Norwich. Her account of her visions of God and especially her understanding of feminine traits in the Godhead have made her writings widely read in modern times.

Ignatius Loyola (1491–1556). After serving as a soldier he had a series of spiritual experiences that led him and six companions to vow life-long poverty and service to others. In 1540 the group was constituted as the Society of Jesus, dedicated to rekindling Christian commitment and to missionary work beyond Europe. The Jesuits (as they were known) elected him their first 'General'. They later engaged widely in education.

Teresa of Avila (1515–82), Spanish mystic and Carmelite nun who, like her contemporary St John of the Cross, was a poet and spiritual writer. Her influence has been described as 'epoch-making', because she was the first to examine various states of prayer between meditation and ecstasy.

St John of the Cross (1542–91), Spanish mystic whose poems are said to be some of the greatest in Spanish. A Carmelite monk, he was dissatisfied with the laxity of the Order and, in the face of much hostility, sought its reform. His writings deal vividly with spiritual experiences, especially the 'night of the senses' and the 'night of the spirit'.

Mother Teresa of Calcutta (1910–97). An Albanian born in Macedonia, she founded the Missionaries of Charity, who work in Calcutta, principally with dying children in the slums of the city.

Thomas Merton (1915–68). A Trappist monk, who in later years sought the life of a hermit. A member of the community at Gethsemane Abbey in Kentucky, USA, his writings presented monastic spirituality to a wide audience.

Trevor Huddleston (1913–98). An Anglican monk of the Community of the Resurrection, he spent most of his working life in Africa, and was a bold and outspoken opponent of apartheid in South Africa. His book *Naught for Your Comfort* (1956) helped to bring the moral issues involved to a world-wide readership.

Holy Places

Followers of every religion have their 'holy places' to visit – places such as the Buddha's birthplace, the Golden Temple of the Sikhs, Mecca in Saudi Arabia, and the Temple Mount and the Western Wall in Jerusalem. Christian pilgrimages began within three centuries of the crucifixion, though there is evidence that from even earlier times groups of Christians would visit the empty tomb of Jesus. Helena, the mother of the emperor Constantine, visited the Holy Land in 326 CE and founded basilicas (large Christian churches) on the Mount of Olives and in Bethlehem, to mark the birthplace of Jesus.

Today the Holy Land is an obvious and popular place of Christian pilgrimage, but there are many other such sites: Lourdes, Santiago de Compostela, Rome, Assisi, Canterbury, Iona, Lindisfarne and many more draw millions of pilgrim visitors every year.

A pilgrimage is traditionally seen as an exercise of discipline and devotion – a journey whose purpose is as much in the travelling as in the arriving.

THE TOP TEN CHRISTIAN HOLY PLACES

Church of the Holy Sepulchre, Jerusalem.

Catholic pilgrims march in a candlelight procession at Lourdes.

Jerusalem: The Church of the Holy Sepulchre is built over the presumed site of the tomb in which Jesus was buried. Pilgrims can enter the narrow cave. The church – the oldest parts of which date back to the fourth century – is shared by no fewer than six different Christian denominations, each of which jealously guards its foothold there. The Mount of Olives and the Garden of Gethsemane where Jesus prayed on the night of his betrayal can also be visited.

Bethlehem: The Church of the Nativity (in Manger Square) is built on the traditional site of the cave where Jesus was born. Visitors can enter the cave, but the church itself is probably too ornately decorated for Western tastes.

Galilee: The lake where Jesus preached and his followers fished. At its north end are the ruins of the ancient village of Capernaum, where he began his ministry.

Rome: In the massive church of St Peter are the presumed burial places of the two great apostles, Peter and Paul, which have been objects of pilgrimage since the Middle Ages. Tradition says that they were both martyred in Rome in the sixties CE.

Assisi: The birthplace of St Francis and the town where he founded his Franciscan Order in the early thirteenth century, following a dramatic conversion experience. St Clare is also honoured in Assisi, where her 'Poor Clares' Order followed the Franciscan rule of poverty. The basilica of St Francis is a magnificent building, now restored after damage during an earthquake. It houses the tomb of Francis.

Lourdes: Near this French town a 14-year-old peasant girl, Bernadette Soubirous, had a series of visions of the Virgin Mary in 1858. A spring appeared, and miraculous healings were reported. As a result, vast crowds began to visit the town, large churches were built and a medical

● SEE ALSO
INSIDE A CHURCH P52-53

centre was established to investigate the nature of the many claimed cures. In recent times many people have visited Lourdes, not so much seeking a cure as an insight into the mystery of suffering.

Santiago de Compostela:

This town in north-west Spain, traditionally supposed to be the burial place of St James the Apostle, has been a centre of pilgrimage since the Middle Ages. James was the first of the apostles to be martyred, in 44 CE, and the 'Compostela' legend is that his body was carried from Jerusalem to Spain. However, in the absence of any historical evidence, the tradition has been generally abandoned.

The western facade of Santiago Cathedral, with a stall selling symbols of camino scallop shells and staffs.

Dionysiu Monastery, Mount Athos, Greece.

Mount Athos: This

peninsula off the coast of Greece has been a monastic centre since the time of St Athanasius the Athonite in the tenth century. There are now twenty different monasteries there. Although undeniably a 'holy place', its attraction as a centre for pilgrimage is limited by the rule that forbids women to enter the peninsula.

Canterbury: This cathedral city in Kent, England, became a major pilgrimage site in the twelfth century after Thomas à Becket, the Archbishop of Canterbury, was hacked to death in his own cathedral by knights who believed they were acting on the king's wishes. Thomas's tomb was a major site of pilgrimage throughout the Middle Ages – a pilgrimage celebrated in Chaucer's *Canterbury Tales*.

Iona: This is a small island off the west coast of Scotland, which was given to St Columba in the sixth century as a base for his missionary work. Its monastery was famous both for its learning and for its artistic achievements. In 1938 a new Iona Community was founded on the island, led by George McLeod, and the old abbey was restored. Since then it has been a centre for pilgrimage, and for people who wish to live in community for short periods. The community is ecumenical, radical and practical, applying the Christian message to issues of conservation, peace and justice.

THE SCALLOP SHELL

Medieval pilgrims to Santiago de Compostela took to wearing a scallop shell as a badge, which gave them admission to monasteries and abbeys on the journey, and also to basic hospitality in people's homes. The badge, worn or carved in stone, became a familiar mark of pilgrimage. In fact, the Swedish word for 'scallop' is literally 'pilgrim-mussel'!

A THOUGHT

Holy places don't make holy people; holy people make holy places.

Saints and Martyrs
HEROES OF THE FAITH

Saints and heroes of the faith didn't cease to exist once the last apostle had died. Even the church's harshest critics would salute such men and women as Dietrich Bonhoeffer (executed by the Nazis), Desmond Tutu, Janani Luwum (put to death by Idi Amin), Oscar Romero (shot dead in his own cathedral in El Salvador), Mother Teresa of Calcutta and Martin Luther King. In their different ways, each was fighting as a Christian for the rights of the poor and powerless. They were not plaster saints; they probably had their share of human frailties and mixed motives. But they were not ashamed to stand alongside the oppressed and to bring, as Jesus did, 'good news to the poor'.

St Elizabeth of Hungary portrayed with a cloak full of roses and carrying bread behind her back to depict her secret almsgiving.

HEROES AND MARTYRS OF THE PAST

A short selection

Ignatius of Antioch: Bishop of Antioch in the period immediately after the apostles, he was killed by lions in the Colosseum in Rome. During the weeks before his death he wrote seven letters to the leaders of various churches.

Adelbert of Prague: Tenth-century bishop and missionary. Spread the Christian faith in Hungary, Bohemia, the Slavic lands and Prussia. Executed as a suspected Polish spy in 997.

Elizabeth of Hungary: Thirteenth-century queen of Hungary, who after her husband's early death became a Franciscan 'tertiary' (that is, keeping a rule of life but not becoming a nun). For the rest of her short life she devoted her time to the relief of the sick, the poor and the elderly. She died aged 24, largely as the result of her austere lifestyle.

Francis of Assisi: In the early thirteenth century, after a vision of Christ, he gave away all his possessions and adopted a life of poverty. The Order he founded, the Franciscans, has remained faithful to this principle of a simple lifestyle, public preaching and a vision of the completeness of the whole creation under God.

Clare: A contemporary of Francis, who shared his convictions and founded an Order for women on similar lines to the Franciscans: the Minoresses or Poor Clares.

Vincent de Paul: French parish priest in the seventeenth century, who devoted his life to the poor and oppressed. He founded the Vincentian Congregation, and also the Sisters of Charity, for work in the slums of Europe. His priests travelled to Poland, Ireland and Scotland with the same commitment to the needy.

Seraphim of Sarov: Eighteenth-century Russian visionary, monk and hermit. He came to represent Russian spirituality in its most pure form, with great emphasis on the source of true light, and of poverty as a way of life. He was found dead in his cell in January 1833.

William Carey: English Baptist missionary, whose vision of world-wide evangelism gave birth to the foundation of the Baptist Missionary Society in 1792. He himself served in Bengal from 1794 to 1829. He played a leading part in the campaign for the abolition of *suti* (the burning of widows on their husband's funeral pyres). He died in 1834.

Portrait of Vincent de Paul by Sebastien Bourdon.

● SEE ALSO
DISTINGUISHED MONKS AND
NUNS P42-43

HEROES AND MARTYRS OF MORE MODERN TIMES

Mary Slessor: Scottish missionary to Calabar, Nigeria, where she first went in 1876, aged 28. Her special concern was for babies and children, rescuing many from poverty and disease. She penetrated the dangerous Okoyong area and settled among its people for many years. She died in 1915.

Gladys Aylward: Englishwoman who felt a call to serve as a missionary while working as a parlour maid in London. Turned down by the China Inland Mission for educational reasons, she used her life savings to travel to Yunchen, in Shanxi Province in China. As a freelance missionary, she worked with children and families, eventually rescuing 94 children from the invading Japanese by leading them across the mountains – a feat re-created in the film *The Inn of the Sixth Happiness*. She died in Taipei in 1970.

Dietrich Bonhoeffer: German Lutheran pastor, born in 1906. In the 1930s he openly criticized Hitler's regime. Forbidden by the Nazi government from teaching and banned from Berlin, he was part of a group who sought links with the British government in their opposition to Hitler. He was arrested in 1943 and hanged in 1945.

Maximilian Kolbe: Polish Franciscan monk. Arrested by the Gestapo in 1941 for providing shelter and escape for Jewish and other refugees in Poland, he was transferred to Auschwitz and held in one of the notorious 'bunkers'. A man from his bunker was thought to have escaped, and the guards seized ten prisoners at random as a reprisal. They were to be starved to death. One of the men pleaded for mercy, crying for his wife and children. Father Kolbe offered to take his place. He survived two weeks of starvation and was then executed by lethal injection. He was canonized (recognized as a saint of the church) in 1981.

Janani Luwum: Anglican Archbishop of Uganda in the 1970s, who opposed the tyrannical reign of President Idi Amin. His criticism was effective in drawing world attention to the plight of many Ugandans, but it enraged Amin, who arranged for the archbishop to be killed in a car crash in 1977.

Gladys Aylward photographed in 1957.

Statue and painting of Maximilian Kolbe in a church at Nagasaki, Japan.

A carving over the entrance to Westminster Abbey, London, commemorates some martyrs of modern times. From left to right: Janani Luwum, Elizabeth of Russia, Martin Luther King, Oscar Romero and Dietrich Bonhoeffer.

The Missionaries
Into All the World

Jesus told his followers to 'make disciples of all nations' (Matthew 28:19) and from the very first they set out to do just that. From the time when Europe had been effectively 'Christianized', however, the command of Jesus seems to have been largely forgotten, and it was not until the Spanish, Italian, Portuguese and Dutch explorers in the fifteenth and sixteenth centuries discovered new lands across the seas that things began to change.

Jesuit missionaries – members of the Society of Jesus, a religious order formed following the Reformation – were at the forefront of a new movement to take the church's message to distant shores. It was some time before the relatively new Protestant churches caught the same vision, but when they did, it sparked an astonishing explosion of missionary activity that saw churches planted in Asia, Africa and the Far East, changing the map of Christendom for ever.

The story is one of amazing courage, initiative and faith. Modern commentators tend to see it as part of a programme of colonization, but for those taking part it was simply a way of carrying out a clear Christian responsibility to share with others what God had shared with them.

The Command of Jesus

'But you will receive power when the Holy Spirit has come upon you; and you will be my witnesses in Jerusalem, in all Judea and Samaria, and to the ends of the earth.'
ACTS 1:8

What People Have Said About Missionaries

• • • • • • • • • • • •

'God had an only Son, and he was a missionary and a physician.'
DAVID LIVINGSTONE

'The Spirit of Christ is the spirit of missions, and the nearer we get to him the more intensely missionary we must become.'
HENRY MARTYN

'We are the children of the converts of foreign missionaries; and fairness means that I must do to others as men once did to me.'
MALTBIE D. BABCOCK

'The church exists by mission as fire exists by burning.'
EMIL BRUNNER

'The believer cannot be restrained. He betrays himself. He confesses and teaches this gospel to the people at the risk of life itself.'
MARTIN LUTHER

Time Chart

By the end of the second century:
Christianity was established in North Africa.

By the end of the fourth century:
Christianity was the recognized religion of the whole Roman empire. There were also Christian churches in Nubia and Ethiopia.

By the end of the seventh century:
Christianity had been largely driven out of Africa by the Arab wars and the rise of Islam.

In the sixteenth century:
The Pope gave authority to Spanish and Portuguese explorers to evangelize the territories they 'discovered', with the assistance of priests who travelled with them. Much of Latin America was 'Christianized'. Portuguese missions had planted churches in the Congo and Angola.

The Jesuits launched missions in India, Indonesia and Japan, where they faced opposition but also made converts.

The Jesuit missionary St Francis Xavier, baptizing a Mexican Indian. Painting by Juan Rodriguez Juarez.

Memorial in Nagasaki commemorating the crucifixion of 26 Christians – six of them European missionaries – in Japan in 1597.

● SEE ALSO
CHRISTIANITY IN THE MODERN
WORLD P120-121
DISCIPLES P28-29

Count Nicolaus von Zinzendorf (1700 – 1760) was an influential figure in the Moravian Church and supported its establishment in America.

In the seventeenth century:
The English and Dutch began to create churches in India for their own expatriates who lived and worked there.

In the eighteenth century:
Protestant missionary work in India (mostly English and Dutch) began in earnest.

In the nineteenth century:
Evangelical and Protestant missions were launched on an almost world-wide basis. At first most of the missionaries were from Britain and then continental Europe, but American missions soon joined in strongly. Africa became a major scene of missionary activity, and there were also missions to China and other parts of the Far East.

Book illustration of C. W. M. Ellis preaching to local people in Hawaii, about 1826.

In the twentieth century:
Most of the churches in former 'missionary' areas acquired local leadership and self-government. Churches in Africa grew enormously.

In the twenty-first century:
The major emphasis of Christian mission has been to reach remote tribal peoples (through such organizations as the Wycliffe Bible Translators) or to re-evangelize the increasingly secular societies of the West.

Statue of David Livingstone, missionary, explorer and slave-trade adversary, at Victoria Falls, Zimbabwe.

Some Facts About Mission Today

China: The first missionaries to China were from the Eastern Orthodox Church in the seventh century and the churches they founded survived until about the fourteenth century. The first Western missionaries arrived in the thirteenth century, but it was not until the Jesuit missions 300 years later that a Christian community was formed. Eventually the Jesuits incurred the wrath of the emperor, and Christianity was banned in China. It returned in the nineteenth century, when the first Protestant missionaries landed. Today, following years of struggle under the Chinese 'Cultural Revolution', the Christian churches of China are growing rapidly.

India: There is evidence that Christianity existed in India as early as the fifth century, but real growth awaited the arrival of European missionaries, first in the fifteenth and then (the Jesuits) in the sixteenth centuries. Protestant missionaries followed the opening up of trade with the East. Today the Christian churches represent the second largest minority religion in India, comprising about 2.5 per cent of the population.

Africa: The part of Africa bordering the Mediterranean was evangelized in the early days of Christianity, as was Egypt and then Nubia and Ethiopia (where the Orthodox Church is still strong). Following the advent of Islam most of North Africa was lost to the church and it was not until the great missionary movement of the nineteenth century that sub-Saharan Africa was evangelized. Since then, and increasingly since the churches adopted African (rather than expatriate) leadership, the growth of the church in the continent has been phenomenal.

What is a 'Church'?
BUILDING OR 'BODY'?

A minister was woken by the police at three in the morning, to be told that his church had been completely destroyed by fire. 'No, it hasn't,' he said. 'They're all asleep in bed.' Both he and the police had used the word 'church' correctly, in the dictionary sense, but they meant quite different things by it. In common usage a 'church' is a building, but in its biblical meaning the word describes a community, not a construction – people, rather than bricks and mortar.

The Nicene Creed says that Christians believe in 'one holy, catholic and apostolic Church'. The church of Christ is intended to be one, rather than many; holy, rather than worldly; catholic (from the Greek word for 'universal') to show that it is all-embracing; and apostolic, because it follows the teaching and example of Christ's apostles. There are consequently many churches, in towns and villages all over the world, but only one church, to which, in the deepest sense, every Christian belongs.

How It All Began

When Jesus asked his disciples who they would say he was, Peter (presumably answering for them all) said that he was the Messiah of God. Jesus told Peter that his heavenly Father had revealed that truth to him, and that it would be on this 'rock' that he would build his church (Matthew 16:15–18). The word for 'church' that he used means 'assembly' or 'gathering', and from the start it was seen in that way. After the resurrection the disciples 'gathered' together, and after Pentecost the new believers 'gathered' into a community of faith.

For a long while – perhaps two centuries – Christians had no dedicated buildings of their own. The church met in people's houses or in hired rooms, like the schoolroom in which the first believers in Ephesus met with Paul (Acts 19:9). Only when they began to realize that the Second Coming might be long delayed did Christians feel it appropriate to construct and own church buildings.

'IN CHRIST'

The apostle Paul used the phrase 'in Christ' to denote those who were true members of the 'body of Christ', the church. So he would address those who were Christians in Colosse, for example, as 'the saints and faithful brothers and sisters in Christ in Colosse' (Colossians 1:2). They were 'in Colosse' geographically, but they were 'in Christ' spiritually.

LIKE A RIVER

'The church is like a river. In the last book of the Bible, John the Visionary sees a huge throng of people from every nation, kindred, tribe and tongue coming together in a great chorus of praise. Like the river, they have all started in different places, but have now brought their different streams into a single flow. The image of the river reminds us forcibly that, though the church consists by definition of people from the widest possible variety of backgrounds, part of the point of it all is that they belong to one another, and are meant to be part of the same powerful flow, going now in the same single direction. Diversity gives way to unity.'

TOM WRIGHT, BISHOP OF DURHAM

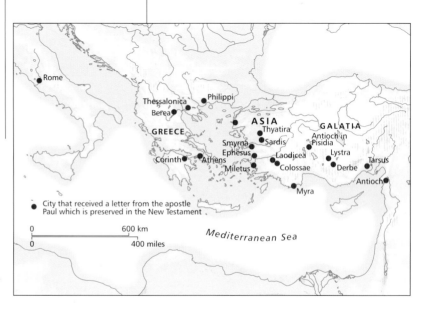

City that received a letter from the apostle Paul which is preserved in the New Testament

0   600 km
0   400 miles

Mediterranean Sea

Cities featured in the New Testament accounts of the travels of the apostle Paul.

● SEE ALSO
BELONGING P90-91
BREAD AND WINE P92-93
DISCIPLES P28-29
HOW THE FIRST CHRISTIANS DID IT P34

MARKS OF THE CHURCH

■ The church of Christ is built on the confession of Peter that Jesus is 'the Messiah, the Son of the living God' (Matthew 16:16).

■ Its distinguishing feature is faith in Jesus Christ.

■ Its badge of membership is baptism.

■ It is intended to carry on the work and witness that Jesus began on earth: 'As the Father has sent me, so I send you' (John 20:21).

■ Its commission is to 'make disciples of all nations' (Matthew 28:19).

■ Its members are to share in the 'breaking of bread', as commanded by Jesus: 'Do this in remembrance of me' (1 Corinthians 11:24).

■ It is to share Christ's concern for the poor, the marginalized and the weak.

■ Its calling is to 'proclaim the mighty acts of him who called you out of darkness into his marvellous light' (1 Peter 2:9).

What People Have Said About the Church

'Where three are gathered together, there is a church, even though they be laymen.'
TERTULLIAN

'Wherever we see the Word of God purely preached and heard, there a Church of God exists, even if it swarms with many faults.'
JOHN CALVIN

'While God waits for his temple to be built of love, men bring stones.'
RABINDRANATH TAGORE

'The Christian Church is the one organization in the world that exists purely for the benefit of non-members.'
WILLIAM TEMPLE

'The Church is the family of God. It is seen in miniature in each family.'
JOHN FERGUSON

One aspect of the work of the church is to bring the message of Jesus to people on the outside. Here a street preacher challenges his audience at Hyde Park in London.

Christians are found in every nation and come from every walk of life. A crowd gathers round a wooden cross in a street in Marseille, France.

THE BODY OF CHRIST

One of the most vivid metaphors for the church in the New Testament is that of the 'body'. The apostle Paul put it like this: 'For just as the body is one and has many members, and all the members of the body, though many, are one body, so it is with Christ. For in the one Spirit we were all baptized into one body – Jews or Greeks, slaves or free – and we were all made to drink of one Spirit' (1 Corinthians 12:12).

Inside a Church
OBJECTS AND OBJECTIVES

Most people are familiar with the outside of a church, whether it's a traditional one with a spire or tower, or a more modern one. To many, however, the inside of a church is not familiar. It feels dark (especially if it's got stained glass windows) and there's often a strange smell compounded of damp, floor polish, old books and sometimes incense. They like to see the building on the street corner, or at the heart of their town or village – it's a reassuring presence. But it's often only on holiday, especially in a foreign country, that they venture inside.

In fact, the inside of a church building reflects every aspect of the Christian faith and the way its followers practise it, from the baptism that marks the beginning of faith to the funeral that marks the end of their earthly life. All human life is here, which makes a visit to a church one of the most rewarding – and sometimes profoundly moving – experiences.

What to Find in a Church

- The building usually faces east, so a major feature is the east window.

- The font will often be found near the door. It is a receptacle for water for baptism.

- The central part of the church is the nave, running from west to east.

- The nave is often traversed by the transept, a crossing that creates a cruciform shape for the church.

- At the east end of the church is the chancel (where the ministers and choir sit).

- Often on either side of the chancel there will be a pulpit, from which a sermon or homily is delivered, and the lectern, from which the Bible is read.

- Beyond the chancel, at the east end of the church, the sanctuary is to be found. Here, traditionally, the holy table or altar is placed, though in many churches today this has been relocated to the nave to make it more central and visible for the congregation.

- In the sanctuary there may be an aumbry or 'tabernacle' (for the reserved sacrament) and a sanctuary lamp, which is lit when the sacrament is present in the aumbry.

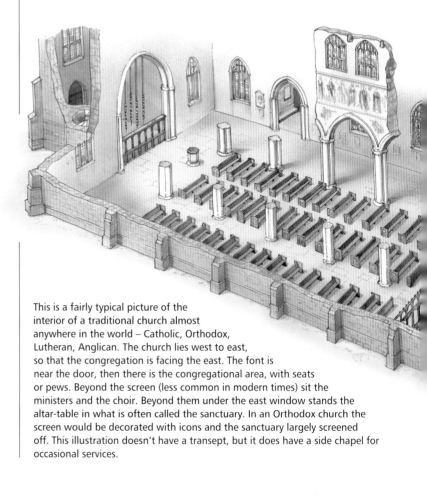

This is a fairly typical picture of the interior of a traditional church almost anywhere in the world – Catholic, Orthodox, Lutheran, Anglican. The church lies west to east, so that the congregation is facing the east. The font is near the door, then there is the congregational area, with seats or pews. Beyond the screen (less common in modern times) sit the ministers and the choir. Beyond them under the east window stands the altar-table in what is often called the sanctuary. In an Orthodox church the screen would be decorated with icons and the sanctuary largely screened off. This illustration doesn't have a transept, but it does have a side chapel for occasional services.

Robes and Vestments

In Old Testament times those who led the worship of God and offered the sacrifices wore special robes or vestments. We don't know for sure whether Jesus wore the traditional cloak of a rabbi, but there are suggestions in the Gospels that he did (see Luke 8:44, for instance). It's unlikely that those who led the worship of the first Christian churches, meeting in the open air or in each other's houses, wore special robes, but by the fourth century it became the practice for Christian leaders (bishops, presbyters and deacons, as they were called) to wear distinctive dress while ministering. These robes were based on the ordinary dress of gentlemen of earlier generations, but acquired a religious significance. They are now worn by most priests in the Catholic and Orthodox traditions as well as by Anglicans and Lutherans. Reformed Church ministers tend to wear either a black 'preaching gown' or academic robes, though in many Free and Evangelical churches no special robes or vestments are worn.

THE OPEN CHURCH

'How beautiful to have the church always open, so that every tired wayfaring man may come in and be soothed by all that art can suggest of a better world when he is weary of this.'
RALPH WALDO EMERSON

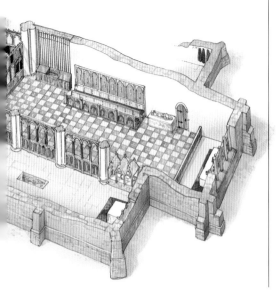

Other Churches

In churches of the Independent or Reformed tradition, the pulpit will be more prominent and the communion table probably less so. Baptist churches will have a baptistery, often at the front of the church, for 'believer's baptism'. There will be no statues or ornaments, other than possibly a simple cross.

Bethania Chapel, Maesteg, South Wales. An example of an interior typical of churches in the Reformed, Independent and Baptist traditions.

Orthodox churches have an iconostasis – a screen decorated with icons – which screens off the sanctuary from the rest of the church.

The 'Communion of Saints'
CROSSING THE GREAT DIVIDE

We have seen that Christians believe in life beyond death, and that that life is lived in a place or condition called 'heaven'. That means that at any given moment there will be many more Christians 'there' than 'here', which leads to the idea of the 'Communion of Saints' – which simply means the fellowship of all Christians who have ever lived, both those alive on earth now, and those who have crossed over into the next life.

Although heaven is a powerful and influential element in the Christian faith, most Christians are prepared to accept that they can know very little about it in advance. They believe that those they love who have died are in an environment that is totally fulfilling, rewarding and joyful. What they also believe, however, is that Christians who have died and those who are still alive are united in this Communion of Saints, a fellowship that embraces the many who are 'there' and the comparatively few who are 'here'. You don't have to be a 'saint' in the formal church sense to belong to it, as long as you are a 'saint' in the biblical sense – a follower of Jesus, on the path that leads to God. In this fellowship Christians who have lost loved ones find encouragement and hope. Though separated by the divide that we call 'death', they still belong together, because they all belong to Christ.

The Gateway to Paradise, detail from *The Last Judgement*, on the western facade of the Voronet Monastery, Moldavia, Romania, 1480.

What is a 'Saint'?

There are two answers to this question. As far as the New Testament is concerned, a 'saint' is simply a Christian. So the apostle Paul writes to the 'saints' at Corinth, even though, as his letter later shows, some of them weren't behaving in a very 'saintly' manner. He actually describes them as 'called to be saints'. In other words, everyone who believes in Jesus has embarked on a spiritual journey that will eventually make them 'holy' (which is what 'saint' actually means).

The second answer concerns the practice of the church, or, more specifically, the Roman Catholic Church. From early times some Christians – those whose lives have reflected Christian virtues or courage in exceptional ways – have been recognized as Saints (with a capital 'S'). They are 'canonized' – that's to say, they get a day in the Church Calendar when they are remembered. It is part of Catholic belief that such people can aid us by their prayers.

Of course, churches in other traditions also honour these great examples of faith, especially those, such as the Virgin Mary and the apostles, whose lives are recorded in the Bible.

A Panorama of Biblical Saints

Peter and Andrew: The first disciples to be called by Jesus (Mark 1:17). Peter was also the first to confess faith in Jesus as the Messiah (Mark 8:29).

James and John: Sons of Zebedee, nicknamed 'Sons of Thunder'. They were disciples and apostles.

Mary: Jesus' mother – told by the angel messenger that she would be the mother of the Messiah, 'the Son of the Most High'. She was present at the crucifixion and also in the upper room when Jesus appeared to his disciples after the resurrection.

Mary Magdalene: A disciple of Jesus, a woman 'out of whom he had cast seven devils' (Luke 8:2). Obviously there had been dark and ugly things in her life, and her intense devotion to Jesus doubtless stemmed from her gratitude for what he had done for her. She was privileged to be the first witness of the risen Jesus.

James: 'the brother of the Lord' (Mark 6:3). He was a leading figure in the early days of the church in Jerusalem and with Peter presided at the Council of Jerusalem in 49 CE. According to Hegesippus in the second century, James was put to death in 62 CE.

Paul: The great missionary to the Gentile people and writer of many of the apostolic letters in the New Testament. Probably executed in Rome in 65 CE.

Stephen: The first Christian martyr. He had been chosen as a 'deacon' to supervise the daily distribution of food (Acts 6, 7). He was stoned to death, possibly in 35 CE.

Prayer and the Communion of Saints

All Christians remember and give thanks for their fellow believers who have died. Christians in the Catholic and Orthodox traditions also believe that it is right and helpful to pray for them, and, where 'saints' and especially the Virgin Mary are concerned, to ask them to pray for us. Protestant Christians feel that to do this is to imply that God's promises of forgiveness and eternal life for those who believe in Jesus are not enough. This issue has been less divisive over the last few decades, partly because the Roman Catholic Church puts far less emphasis on offering masses for the dead, and partly because many Protestants have found ways of including their loved ones who have died in their prayers without directly making requests for them.

What is Heaven Like?

Some of the pictures offered by the Bible

A field from which the weeds have been removed *(Matthew 13:24 – 30)*

A tiny seed which grows into something that can provide shelter for those who need it *(Matthew 13:31, 32)*

A hidden treasure *(Matthew 13:44)*

A pearl of great value *(Matthew 13:45)*

A fishing net that gathers in all kinds of fish *(Matthew 13:47)*

A beautiful city, where death, tears, mourning and crying will have been abolished *(Revelation 21:3, 4)*

A city of golden streets, where the gates are never shut, and people of every race and nation are welcome to enter *(Revelation 21:21 – 25)*

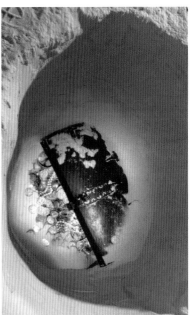

'The kingdom of heaven is like treasure hidden in a field. When a man found it, he hid it again, and then in his joy went out and sold all he had and bought that field.'

SØREN KIERKEGAARD

'God creates out of nothing. Wonderful, you say. Yes, to be sure, but he does what is still more wonderful: he makes saints out of sinners.'

Kierkegaard was a nineteenth-century Danish philosopher and theologian who criticized the 'empty formality' of the Danish church of his time.

The Mother of Jesus
'HAIL, MARY, FULL OF GRACE'

When a young Jewish girl in the village of Nazareth was visited by an angel and told that she was pregnant with the Messiah of Israel, she was shocked and bewildered. 'How can this be?' she asked. 'I am a virgin.' The angel's reply was even more shocking. 'The Holy Spirit will come upon you, and the child to be born will be called the Son of God.' Whatever we make of Luke's account of the 'Annunciation', as it is called, there can be no doubt that the young woman, Mary, was destined to be not only the mother of Jesus, the prophet and Messiah from Galilee, but also the most honoured and revered woman in human history.

The veneration of Mary as the mother of the divine Son of God began early in the history of the church, and became intense in the Middle Ages – to the extent that at times Christianity seemed to be the religion of Mary rather than Jesus. In the Eastern Orthodox churches she is known as *Theotokos*, literally the 'bearer of God', a title that became popular in the fourth century. Although criticized by some, it was upheld at the Councils of Ephesus and Chalcedon in the fifth century.

Candles illuminate a picture of the Virgin and Child in the Bocca della Verita Church, Rome, Italy.

'EXCESSIVE VENERATION'

The Constitution of the Second Vatican Council (1965) warned Roman Catholics against 'excessive veneration' of the Blessed Virgin Mary, while reaffirming the practice of honouring her and seeking her prayers.

The Blessed Virgin Mary in Art

No woman in history, surely, has been depicted in art as much as the mother of Jesus. In iconography, in portraiture, in frescoes and in statuary, artists have found her an endless source of inspiration. Probably no single piece of art captures more profoundly the pathos of the death of Jesus and its impact on his mother than the fifteenth-century *Pieta* by Michelangelo, a carving in marble of Mary cradling the body of her son on her lap.

Pieta by Michelangelo in St Peter's, Rome.

The Coronation of the Virgin in Paradise by Jacobello del Fiore, 1438.

The Virgin Mary in the Gospels

Considering her huge role in Christian history, Mary has a fairly minor one in the Gospels. The stories of the birth of Jesus in Matthew (chapters 1 and 2) and Luke (chapters 1 and 2) give her a prominent place, of course (more so in Luke), but from then on she seems to fade into the background. John relates the miracle of Jesus turning water into wine at Cana, in which Mary had as introductory role (2:4), and Mark describes a strange scene in which Mary and the 'brothers' of Jesus are left outside the house while Jesus tells the people inside that those who believe in him are his true 'mother and brothers' (3:21). John's Gospel describes her standing 'near the cross' and Jesus commending her to the care of his friend John (19:25–27) and Luke names her among the disciples in the Upper Room after the resurrection (Acts 1:14).

Perpetual Virginity

The idea that Mary remained a virgin throughout her life emerged in the church from the fourth century onwards. The evidence of the Gospels could imply that Mary had intercourse after the birth of Jesus, and that he had 'brothers' (see Matthew 1:25 and Mark 3:32), but Catholic scholars interpret the language differently.

Immaculate Conception
This is often confused with Virgin Birth, but is an entirely separate concept. The idea that Mary was born 'without stain of original sin' (that is, 'immaculate') began to take root during the later Middle Ages and was defined by Pope Pius IX in 1854.

The Assumption
This is the belief that Mary did not 'die' (in the sense that her body suffered corruption) but was 'taken up' into heaven, like Elijah (2 Kings 2:11). The Assumption was widely believed in the church from the fifth century onwards, but was not defined until 1950. It is not a dogma of the Orthodox Church, which also rejects the doctrine of the Immaculate Conception. Protestant and Reformed churches, of course, do not hold to the doctrines of the Perpetual Virginity, Immaculate Conception or bodily Assumption of the Blessed Virgin Mary.

VIRGIN BIRTH
All the major Christian churches assent to the doctrine of the 'virgin birth' (or more accurately the 'virginal conception') of Jesus, because it is plainly taught in the Gospels. However, many modern biblical scholars have sought to interpret it in a symbolical or theological way rather than as medical fact. The combination of human and divine in the parentage of Jesus certainly helps in understanding Christian claims about his nature – both 'God and man', as it is often expressed.

THE 'HAIL MARY'
Probably the most-used prayer in Christendom, the 'Hail Mary' is based on the greeting of the angel Gabriel to Mary (Luke 1:28).

Hail Mary, Full of Grace,
The Lord is with thee.
Blessed art thou among women,
and blessed is the fruit of thy womb, Jesus.
Holy Mary, Mother of God,
pray for us sinners now,
and at the hour of death.
Amen.

Peter and Paul
THE FISHERMAN AND THE PHARISEE

Jesus, straight from his baptism by John in the River Jordan, is walking beside Lake Galilee. He sees two young fishermen casting a net into the water, and he calls to them, 'Follow me!' They abandon their task, and simply follow him. One of the two men was Simon, later renamed Peter, which means 'the Rock'.

About seven years later, an educated Jewish leader is riding towards Damascus. He carries with him letters authorizing him to arrest and imprison any Christians whom he finds there. Suddenly there is a blinding light from the sky and he hears a voice. 'Why are you persecuting me?' it asks. 'Who are you?' the man responds. 'I am Jesus, whom you are persecuting,' it replies. In obedience to the voice, the man, temporarily blinded by the light, is led into Damascus, where a Christian prays with him, restores his sight and then baptizes him. The Jewish leader, a Pharisee, was Saul of Tarsus, who now took a new name as a Christian – Paul.

Peter and Paul: the names are synonymous with the birth of Christianity. Peter was the first to preach the resurrection of Jesus to the crowds of Jews in Jerusalem at Pentecost. He was also the first to share that same good news with a group of Gentiles in the home of the centurion, Cornelius (Acts 10). So he was the first to 'open the gates of the kingdom' to both Jews and Gentiles. Paul was the first great missionary of the church, travelling thousands of miles across the Mediterranean to preach the gospel and plant churches. Between them, they were more responsible than any other human being for the emergence of Christianity as a powerful force in the Roman world. Tradition has it that both men were martyred in Rome and buried there.

The Fisherman

Peter was without doubt the leader of the twelve apostles. He is always named first in the lists of their names in the Gospels; he is generally their spokesman; and despite his abject denial that he even knew Jesus in the palace of the high priest (Mark 14:71), he is later commissioned by Jesus to 'feed his sheep' (John 21:17). He was the 'lead preacher' on the Day of Pentecost (Acts 2:14) and took the leadership role at the first 'Council' of the Church in Jerusalem (Acts 15:7).

There is a strong tradition that Peter eventually became the leader of the church in Rome, that he was a primary source for Mark's Gospel and that he was martyred in the city under the emperor Nero in about 64 CE. He is the author of the first letter bearing his name in the New Testament, and a probable source for some of the second one, usually dated some time after his death.

Successors of Peter?

That Peter led the church in Rome is widely accepted, as is his apostolic authority there, probably exercised as the church's 'bishop'. Subsequently the church at Rome, and its bishops, were accorded special status in church councils, leading to a claim for the bishop of Rome to be recognized as the 'first among equals' of the bishops. Eventually, by about the sixth century, the 'successor of Peter' was called the 'Pope' and began to exercise authority over other provinces of the church. It was this claim to authority that led to the split with the Eastern Church.

The claim to this special role for the successor of Peter is based on the words of Jesus to Peter in Matthew 16:18, 19: 'And I tell you, you are Peter, and on this rock I will build my church.'

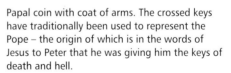

Papal coin with coat of arms. The crossed keys have traditionally been used to represent the Pope – the origin of which is in the words of Jesus to Peter that he was giving him the keys of death and hell.

The Pharisee

Paul described himself as a 'zealous Pharisee', a member of the strictest of the Jewish sects. This makes his conversion on the road to Damascus all the more unexpected and dramatic – people still describe a sudden conversion or change of heart as a 'Damascus road experience'. In fact, there are hints that he was already beginning to have doubts about his hard-line opposition to the followers of Jesus – the 'voice' said that he was finding it hard to 'kick against the goads' (Acts 26:14).

The conversion of such a high-profile and scholarly Jew was a turning point for the emerging church. His letters to the various churches that he planted set out for the first time what we could call a 'Christian theology'. They aren't necessarily easy reading, but they provide an intellectual base for the Christian faith to which people have appealed all down the centuries, from Augustine (fourth century) to Luther (sixteenth) to John Wesley (eighteenth) to Karl Barth (twentieth).

Paul travelled hundreds of miles on foot, and also made long sea journeys across the Mediterranean to reach new regions with his message. Part of his journey to Rome was on board a grain ship.

Paul and Jesus

In recent times some people have suggested that Paul took the 'simple' message of Jesus as it is found in the Gospels and turned it into a complex series of doctrines, including the idea that Jesus is divine. This seems extremely unlikely given that two of the authors of the Gospels, Mark and Luke, were close associates of his and presumably approved of the message he was preaching.

Famous Words of Peter and Paul

Peter

Therefore let the entire house of Israel know with certainty that God has made him both Lord and Messiah, this Jesus whom you crucified.
ACTS 2:36

But you are a chosen race, a royal priesthood, a holy nation, God's own people, in order that you may proclaim the mighty acts of him who called you out of darkness into his marvellous light.
1 PETER 2:9

Finally, all of you, have unity of spirit, sympathy, love for one another, a tender heart, and a humble mind.
1 PETER 3:8

Paul

Love is patient; love is kind; love is not envious or boastful or arrogant or rude. It does not insist on its own way; it is not irritable or resentful; it does not rejoice in wrongdoing, but rejoices in the truth. It bears all things, believes all things, hopes all things, endures all things. Love never ends.
1 CORINTHIANS 13:5–7

And now faith, hope, and love abide, these three; and the greatest of these is love.
1 CORINTHIANS 13:13

For I am convinced that neither death, nor life, nor angels, nor rulers, nor things present, nor things to come, nor powers, nor height, nor depth, nor anything else in all creation, will be able to separate us from the love of God in Christ Jesus our Lord.
ROMANS 8:38, 39

The Vatican, view towards St Peter's, the centre of the Catholic faith. The current Basilica, begun in 1506, took over a century to build. On religious occasions the Pope appears on a balcony above the square to bless the crowds.

Leadership

POPES AND PARSONS

Jesus told his followers very sternly that they were not to worry about status or power: his best leaders would be followers and those who wanted to be 'great' must be servants of the rest (Mark 10:44). So it is strange that many of the most bitter arguments in the Christian church have been about the role and status of its leaders and ministers.

From its earliest days the church has had leaders, of course. First of all there were the apostles, unique as Christ's 'special messengers'. They in turn appointed leaders in the churches that resulted from their preaching of the Christian message. They called these leaders 'elders' or 'overseers', and they in turn were assisted by 'deacons'. Before the death of the last apostle, we can begin to see the shape of the ministry that became normal in the church of the following centuries, with bishops (overseers) as the chief ministers, assisted by presbyters (elders) and deacons.

An army is only as good as its officers, and the history of the church since then has reflected the quality of its leadership. Great men and women have shaped that history – and so, sadly, have some who ignored the warnings of Jesus and were more concerned with status and power than the kingdom of God.

What the New Testament Says About Leadership

'You call me Teacher and Lord – and you are right, for that is what I am. So if I, your Lord and Teacher, have washed your feet, you also ought to wash one another's feet. For I have set you an example, that you also should do as I have done to you. Very truly, I tell you, servants are not greater than their master, nor are messengers greater than the one who sent them.'
JESUS IN JOHN 13:13

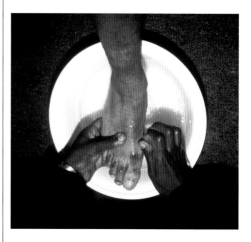

Jesus called the twelve, and said to them, 'Whoever wants to be first must be last of all and servant of all.'
MARK 9:35

Not many of you should become teachers, my brothers and sisters, for you know that we who teach will be judged with greater strictness.
JAMES 3:1

Now a bishop must be above reproach, married only once, temperate, sensible, respectable, hospitable, an apt teacher, not a drunkard, not violent but gentle, not quarrelsome, and not a lover of money. He must manage his own household well, keeping his children submissive and respectful in every way – for if someone does not know how to manage his own household, how can he take care of God's church?
1 TIMOTHY 3:2–4

John Wesley

THE PASTOR PLEADS WITH HIS FLOCK

'One design you are to pursue to the end of time – the enjoyment of God in time and in eternity. Desire other things, so far as they tend to this. Love the creature as it leads to the Creator. But for every step you take, be this the glorious point that terminates your view. Let every affection, and thought, and word, and work be subordinate to this. Whatever you desire or fear, whatever you seek or shun, whatever you think, speak or do, be it in order to your happiness in God, the sole End, as well as the Source of your being.'
FROM A SERMON BY JOHN WESLEY

Bishops

In the early days of the church the apostles appointed 'overseers' for churches or groups of churches. The word they used is the root of our word 'bishop', but they didn't assume the distinctive functions of a modern bishop until after the apostolic era. Some of the early bishops were to become highly revered in the church for their wisdom and courage – the martyrs Polycarp (bishop of Smyrna) and Ignatius (bishop of Antioch), for example, and Irenaeus, the scholarly bishop of Lyons, perhaps the first great theologian of the post-apostolic church.

Popes

Tradition holds that the apostle Peter was the first leader of the church in Rome. He was certainly acknowledged to be 'first among equals' of the apostles. Possibly because of this, or because it was at the heart of the empire, the church in Rome assumed from early times a special place in matters of authority in the catholic (universal) church. It was only with the further passage of time, however, that the concept of the papacy began to develop, with the bishop of Rome – the 'Pope' (literally, 'father') – having supreme authority in matters of church doctrine and government. This position is based on the claim that as Peter's successor in Rome the succeeding bishops of Rome shared the authority which they believe was given by Jesus to Peter alone (Matthew 16:18). This interpretation of the words of Jesus, and the whole concept of a single human figure of absolute authority in the church, is rejected by Christians in the Orthodox and Protestant traditions.

What People Have Said About Ministry

'The Christian ministry is the worst of all trades, but the best of all professions.'
JOSEPH FORD NEWTON

'A constant danger with priests, even zealous priests, is that they become so immersed in the work of the Lord that they neglect the Lord of the work.'
JOHN PAUL II

'The clergyman is expected to be a kind of human Sunday.'
SAMUEL BUTLER

'The Lord opened unto me that being bred at Oxford or Cambridge was not enough to fit and qualify men to be ministers of Christ.'
GEORGE FOX

TAKE ME TO YOUR LEADER...

Jesus spoke of the church as his 'flock', and sheep need a shepherd. Consequently, every Christian congregation has some form of leadership, whether he or she is called a bishop, priest, minister or pastor. The apostle Paul put it like this: 'The gifts he (the risen Jesus) gave were that some would be apostles, some prophets, some evangelists, some pastors and teachers, to equip the saints for the work of ministry, for building up the body of Christ, until all of us come to the unity of the faith and of the knowledge of the Son of God, to maturity, to the measure of the full stature of Christ' (Ephesians 4:11, 12).

Pope Benedict XVI blesses pilgrims gathered in St Peter's Square during his traditional Christmas blessing, 'Urbi et Orbi' ('To the City and the World'), 25 December 2007.

The Great Divide
WHEN EAST AND WEST FELL OUT

Christians tend to think of the early church as a model of peace, harmony and concord. In fact, being composed of ordinary human beings (like its modern counterpart) it had the usual quota of rows, dissension and splits. Most were disagreements over this or that doctrine of the faith, or were squabbles about authority – who is the greatest? All the warnings of Jesus were quite quickly forgotten.

Happily, most of the individual churches maintained fellowship with each other, and generally speaking, for the first three centuries of its life at least, the church stood united in the face of a sceptical and at times antagonistic world. But from the fourth century onwards, more or less coinciding with the time when the Roman empire began to embrace Christianity as its 'official' religion, tensions increasingly broke out between the churches of the West (the 'old' Roman empire) and those of the East, in the Byzantine empire. Despite many attempts at reconciliation, these tensions finally led to the first major division in the church, as the Eastern churches disassociated themselves from Rome and rejected the authority of the Pope. The consequences were momentous, and the division remains to this day.

What the Orthodox Churches Believe

The Orthodox churches hold the same doctrinal beliefs as the Roman Catholic Church, apart from their rejection of the supreme authority of the Pope and of one word from the Western creed – *filioque* in Latin, 'and the Son' in English. The Western church believes that the Holy Spirit is given 'through the Father and the Son'. The Orthodox regard this concept as an 'innovation', and adhere to the belief that the Holy Spirit proceeds only from the Father. The Orthodox also reject the concept of purgatory and admit baptized babies to communion.

During the years of tension between East and West there were sharp differences over the place of icons (see below), which are greatly valued by the Orthodox as channels of grace. Two Western Councils of the Church in the first millennium denounced them as idolatrous.

The Orthodox churches claim to hold in their entirety the teachings of the first seven Ecumenical Councils of the Church, all held before the 'Great Schism' (split) in 1054.

The Rise of Islam

From the preaching of Muhammad (570–632 CE) a new religion was born, one that claimed the same roots as Judaism and respected Jesus as a great prophet, but saw Muhammad as the final voice of divine revelation. The Arab peoples of the Middle East responded enthusiastically to Islam, as it was called, and this had a profound effect, especially on the church in the Byzantine empire. Both politics and economics were affected, but it was the siege of Constantinople by Muslim armies that brought home how serious the position was for the church. In effect, a Muslim–Byzantine border was established, but later centuries saw that eroded.

The Western church was less anxious about Islam, though North Africa, once a bastion of the faith, fell to the Muslim armies. But Christians and Jews were regarded by Muslims as 'people of the Book' and were allowed freedom to practise their religion, within certain limits.

Interior of Santa Sophia, Istanbul, built in the fifth century by the emperor Justinian.

● SEE ALSO
CHRISTIANITY AND ISLAM P72-73
WHEN WEST MEETS EAST P70-71

Icons

As soon as you enter an Orthodox church anywhere in the world you will be aware of icons – flat pictures painted in egg tempera usually on wood, but sometimes on mosaic or ivory. These usually depict a saint or patriarch, and their presence and use in Orthodox worship has led at times to charges of blasphemy or idolatry, since icons are representations of people.

An icon painter once explained that he was not painting 'the Virgin Mary', which would break the second commandment, but 'Virgin-Maryness'. In other words, the icon is not a picture of a person, but of an ideal, and is therefore a powerful aid to holiness. For the Orthodox these paintings, created by devout artists in a context of prayer and meditation, are channels of grace and blessing.

Icon painter at work, Mount Athos, Greece.

Some Orthodox Saints

St Basil (fourth century): His teachings and writings largely created the structure and ethos of Orthodox monasticism, which has been retained to this day.

St Melodus Cormes (eighth century): Author of Greek liturgical hymns, particularly to celebrate the Christian feasts.

St Athanasius (eighth century): Abbot of St Catherine's monastery on Mount Sinai.

St Photius (ninth century): Patriarch of Constantinople and leading opponent of Rome over the *filioque* clause in the Creed.

St Nicodemus of the Holy Mountain (eighteenth century): Monk of Mount Athos, spiritual writer. He produced Greek editions of Roman Catholic writers, including Ignatius Loyola.

GREEK AND RUSSIAN

The Orthodox Church was first established in Constantinople, but after the evangelization of Russia in the ninth and tenth centuries Moscow and Kiev also became important centres for the church, and in the sixteenth century Moscow became a Patriarchate in its own right, though still recognizing the historic primacy of the Patriarch of Constantinople. The Eastern Orthodox Church – now often simply identified as 'Greek' – and the Russian Orthodox Church are 'autocephalous' (that is, having independent governing synods), while remaining members of the same communion, along with a number of smaller Orthodox churches.

Constantinople

Constantine the Great built what he called a 'new Rome' to be the greatest city in the Christian world. In fact it became known as Constantinople. It was, and still is, the centre of the Eastern (Orthodox) Church, and the patriarch of Constantinople – one of five patriarchs (effectively archbishops) – eventually claimed the title of 'Ecumenical (universal) Patriarch', much to the displeasure of the Pope. As the split between East and West widened, Constantinople grew in influence, sending missionaries to the Baltic and Slav lands and to Russia, and planting churches there. From this developed the Greek and Russian Orthodox Churches of today, who recognize the primacy of the Ecumenical Patriarch, while denying him the absolute authority in matters of faith exercised by the Pope.

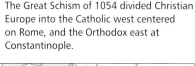

Icon of St Basil, Samos, Greece.

The Great Schism of 1054 divided Christian Europe into the Catholic west centered on Rome, and the Orthodox east at Constantinople.

Catholic in 1054
Orthodox in 1054
● Patriarchate

'Holy' Wars
CRUSADES AND CRUSADERS

Jesus warned his followers that those who take the sword die by the sword (Matthew 26:52), but some of them down the ages have ignored his words and resorted to violence in his name. The most conspicuous example of this is probably the 'Crusades'– wars fought against the Muslims who were infiltrating, and in many cases taking over, the historic Christian sites in the Holy Land. The Crusades, originally proclaimed by Pope Urban II in 1095, lasted on and off for about two hundred years, and in terms of 'liberating' Jerusalem and the holy sites from Muslim control they were a total failure. Several times Jerusalem was recaptured, but always to be lost again. The later Crusades were also aimed at preventing Muslim incursion into the Eastern empire.

Finally popular support in Europe faded, particularly when 'Crusades' seemed to be directed at non-Christians in general and 'heretics' in Western countries.

People in the Crusader Story

Pope Urban II proclaimed the First Crusade in 1095, with the intention of freeing the Church of the Holy Sepulchre from Muslim control and relieving pressure on the Eastern empire.

Bernard of Clairvaux, the monk better known for his mystical and devotional writings, preached in support of the Second Crusade (1147), which was provoked by the fall of the important Syriac-speaking Christian city of Edessa.

Frederick I, Emperor of Germany, **Philip II**, king of France, and **Richard I of England** all took part in the Third Crusade (1189), intended to recover Jerusalem, which had been captured by the Muslim general Saladin in 1187. They failed, and subsequent efforts were diverted to the protection of Constantinople.

Frederick II of Germany actually recovered Jerusalem by negotiation in 1229, but within 20 years it was back in Muslim hands.

Events from the Second Crusade: above, the Council of Acre, and below, the siege by armoured Christian knights of the city of Damascus. From a twelfth-century manuscript by William of Tyre.

'CRUSADE'

The word 'crusade' is of itself anathema to Muslims, as it is based on the French word for being marked with the sign of the cross, and is associated with the military expeditions against Muslims by Christians in the Middle Ages. The word has been used more generally for any energetic and organized campaign with a political, social or religious aim, usually against something (for example, a 'crusade against knife crime'). This reinforces its negative image.

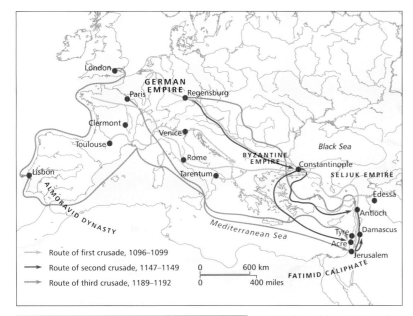

Route of first crusade, 1096–1099
Route of second crusade, 1147–1149
Route of third crusade, 1189–1192

0   600 km
0   400 miles

The Crusader Wars consisted broadly of three campaigns, which together spanned a period of almost a century. A fourth crusade in 1202 was not against the Muslims, but was an attack by Venice on Constantinople in an attempt to deal with a commercial rival.

Aerial view of Acre, besieged by Christian forces in 1190.

Part of the city walls and the Tower of David, Jerusalem.

Christianity Under Islam

Following the Crusades, there was a period when the Christian church and Islam lived alongside each other relatively peacefully. During the Renaissance period, Western scholars were influenced by Islamic philosophy and culture.

The Qur'an gives special status to Judaism and Christianity as Abrahamic faiths, recognizing that all three religions spring from the same roots. However, political and military considerations have often put peaceful coexistence between the three faiths under strain.

CHRISTIAN HOLY SITES

For all the anxieties of the Crusaders, it has to be conceded that the Muslim authorities did a good job in respecting the Christian sites in the Holy Land (many of them built by the Crusaders), largely because their religion accords great respect to the prophet Jesus. However, the later and contentious building of a mosque and dome on the site of the Jewish Temple (revered by Muslims as the place where Abraham was prepared to sacrifice Isaac) is likely to remain an unresolved issue between the two faiths.

THE TEMPLARS

Also known as the 'Knights Templar' or the 'Poor Knights of Christ', they were a major military Order in medieval Christendom. The first nine members bound themselves by a vow in 1119 to protect pilgrims on the public highways of the Holy Land, and were given quarters on the Temple site in Jerusalem. Their Rule, possibly drawn up by Bernard of Clairvaux, was approved by the Council of Troyes in 1129, and they soon acquired both influence and wealth throughout Europe, where they were trusted as bankers. However, that very wealth proved their ruin, because Philip IV of France wanted to get his hands on it and brought charges – generally admitted subsequently to be false – which led to Pope Clement V suppressing the Order in 1312.

A twelfth-century Templar Crusader chapel at Lanleff, Brittany, France, based on the Church of the Holy Sepulchre in Jerusalem.

The Reformation
THE SECOND GREAT DIVIDE

The church of the late Middle Ages – say, from 1000 to 1500 – was an astonishing blend of the deeply spiritual and the seriously sinful. Alongside such giants of the devotional life as Bernard of Clairvaux, Hildegard of Bingen, Julian of Norwich and Francis of Assisi, there were monasteries full of indulgence and even moral corruption. There were some good Popes, some indifferent ones and one or two who were little short of wicked. The church was effectively a political empire of which the Pope was president, wielding enormous power, wealth and authority over the whole of western Europe. Kings and princes felt helpless in the face of possible excommunication, while the ordinary people, in a superstitious age, were in awe of a power that not only controlled much of their daily lives but could also determine their eternal destiny. The sale of indulgences – papal documents promising remission of time in purgatory – and the acquiring of relics, whether genuine or bogus, had more to do with financial returns than spiritual benefits.

There was a general feeling that things couldn't go on like this. Various movements had arisen in protest at abuses within the church – the Lollards in England, the Hussites in Czechoslovakia – but something more was needed than mere protest. In the early sixteenth century, that 'something' appeared, and the second great division in the Christian church was born.

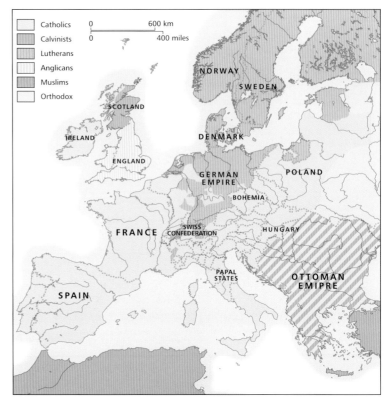

The spiritual division of Europe in 1648. Initial gains were made early in the sixteenth century by Calvinism in France, and Lutheranism in Austria, Poland and Hungary. But by the end of the Thirty Years' War, Catholicism was regaining control of much of central and eastern Europe.

Monument to John Huss outside the Church of Our Lady, Prague, Czech Republic.

A PASSAGE FOR THE WORD

'Whatever resistance we see today offered by almost all the world to the progress of the truth, we must not doubt that our Lord will come at last to break through all the undertakings of men and make a passage for his word.'

JOHN CALVIN

Martin Luther

Luther was an Augustinian monk and professor of biblical exegesis in Wartburg, Germany, who questioned a number of the practices of the medieval church. Protected by various German princes, he felt able to challenge the Vatican on such issues as the sale of indulgences, and then with growing confidence the primacy of the Pope and the infallibility of General Councils of the church. At the same time, partly from his study of the writings of St Augustine, he rejected the medieval church's emphasis on 'good works' as a means to salvation, arguing that we are 'justified' before God solely on the grounds of his

Statue of Martin Luther in Wittenberg, Germany.

grace, received by faith. It was this doctrine of 'justification by faith' that became the distinctively Lutheran contribution to the Reformation, as the movement for change in the church became known. The Lutheran Church became the dominant religious influence in Germany and Scandinavia, and had a profound influence on the English Reformers.

HENRY VIII AND CRANMER

Meanwhile, England had its own version of the Reformation, largely made possible by a rather sordid squabble between the king, Henry VIII, and the Pope over the monarch's multiple marriages. The effect of this rift was to enable reform-minded clergy to introduce ideas that Henry, a staunch Catholic in his theology, would otherwise have banned. After his death, under Edward VI, the Archbishop of Canterbury, Thomas Cranmer, introduced a new Prayer Book along 'Protestant' lines, though retaining Catholic order (bishops, priests and deacons). After Queen Mary's unsuccessful attempts to reverse the Reformation in England, Elizabeth's reign ensured that its future became secure. Like the Lutheran Church, the Church of England and the many other churches that would grow from it around the world sought to provide a 'middle way' between Roman Catholicism and Reformed Protestantism.

Portrait of English King Henry VIII by Hans Holbein the Younger.

ZWINGLI AND CALVIN

Following Luther's reformation movement in Germany, there were repercussions elsewhere. In Switzerland two theologians went further than Luther.

Ulrich Zwingli rejected any notion that in the Eucharist there was anything more than an act of memorial of the death of Jesus: the bread and wine were symbols, not sacraments. Later, an even more influential scholar emerged in Switzerland.

John Calvin was a French Reformer and theologian. He shared many of Luther's beliefs, especially on the authority of Scripture and the doctrine of justification by grace through faith, but he went further than the German Reformer, stressing the principle that God takes the sole initiative in human salvation and diluting what he saw as Luther's 'catholic' beliefs about the Eucharist. Under threat, he fled from France, first to Basle and then to Germany, returning to Switzerland when the civil authorities welcomed him back to Geneva. His distinctive teaching was predestination: our salvation is determined not by our choices, but by God's sovereign choice. This doctrine was given the name 'Calvinism' and became the driving force of the Reformation in parts of Germany, the Netherlands and Scotland.

Ulrich Zwingli, leader of the Protestant Reformation in Switzerland, killed in battle in 1531.

John Calvin, theologian and Reformer, who gave his name to a particularly strict version of Protestantism.

One Church, Divided
THE RISE OF DENOMINATIONS

As we have seen, the split between East and West was the first, but by no means the last, in the history of Christianity. As a direct result of the Reformation, for the first time since the Great Schism in 1054 the all-pervasive power of Rome was challenged. The vast religious and political empire that had encompassed the whole of western Europe was shaken.

Out of those stormy years new churches emerged, the churches of the 'Reformation'. They were known as 'Protestant' because they 'protested' against the authority of Rome and for the authority of the Bible. Building on widespread concern about abuses within the church – the selling of 'indulgences', for instance, and corruption in some monastic houses – a new age was ushered in, one in which there would no longer be only one visible church, but many, even though all claimed to be part of the universal church founded by Christ.

The Reformation also had a profound effect on the Roman Catholic Church. What was called the 'Counter-Reformation' saw the church reinvigorated, its disciplines re-imposed, abuses checked and the authority of the Pope reasserted. Western Europe no longer could be seen as a 'Holy Roman empire', but from Rome's point of view the damage caused by the Reformers was at least contained.

One of the pre-Reformation movements which concerned the Catholic hierarchy were the Cathars, who flourished in south-west France. Condemned as heretics, their power was eventually broken when their principal stronghold at Montsegur was besieged.

The Fracture of 'Christendom'

With the onset of the Renaissance (the rebirth of learning in the late Middle Ages), voices were raised in protest at both obvious abuses in the church and the supreme authority of the bishop of Rome. In England John Wycliffe preached the urgent need for reform in the fourteenth century. He questioned papal infallibility and the doctrine of transubstantiation. His ideas greatly influenced John Huss, a priest and theologian in Bohemia. Huss was eventually burnt at the stake for heresy, but a Reform movement had begun in Bohemia that anticipated the subsequent reformist events led by people like Martin Luther a century later. Cracks were appearing in the hitherto impregnable Holy Roman empire.

John Wycliffe, fourteenth-century English religious Reformer. Wycliffe embarked on a translation of the Bible into English in order to bypass the established church and make the word of God accessible to all literate people.

● SEE ALSO
THE REFORMATION P66-67

The Counter-Reformation

Reform movements began in the Roman Catholic Church at much the same time as Martin Luther was leading many German churches away from allegiance to Rome. The newly formed Order of the Jesuits (The Society of Jesus) provided the intellectual ammunition, becoming deeply involved in the situation in Germany, and then elsewhere as Reformation ideas spread. The Council of Trent in 1562–63 reasserted the authority of the Pope over those Catholics who looked for some level of reconciliation with the Protestants. The greatest triumph of the Counter-Reformation was to bring the churches of southern Germany and Poland back into the Catholic fold.

General Congregation of the Council of Trent, painted by Elijah Naurizio.

DENOMINATIONS

'Denominations' simply means 'name groups', and in modern times the word has been used to describe different groups of Christians formed into associations of churches. Since the Reformation, the Protestant section of Christendom has given birth to a bewildering array of such denominations, reflecting every possible variation of orthodox Christian belief and practice.

Lutheran: The church that arose from the teaching and leadership of Martin Luther, the first of the great Reformers of the church. Its distinguishing doctrine is justification by faith through God's grace. Lutherans are particularly strong in northern Europe and the USA.

Presbyterian: These churches generally follow the teaching of John Calvin, the French/Swiss Reformer who took a more radical line than Luther. The supremacy of Scripture, the initiative of God in our salvation, simplicity of worship, and leadership exercised by both lay and ordained people are its distinguishing marks.

Anglican: The Anglican churches are probably closest to the Lutherans, especially in maintaining the key elements of Catholic order within a framework of Protestant doctrine. Beginning in the British Isles, Anglicanism now constitutes a world-wide communion of autonomous churches linked to the Archbishop of Canterbury.

Baptist: This movement began in Amsterdam in 1609, with the baptism of a number of adult believers. Baptists believe that baptism is an adult response to the gospel, requiring an informed faith. Baptist churches have been particularly effective in missionary work across the world.

Congregational: These churches – also known as 'independent' or 'Reformed' churches – locate church authority in the local congregation, which orders worship, appoints pastors, establishes the church's doctrinal beliefs and manages its funds.

Methodist: The Methodist Church came into being through the preaching of John Wesley who, as a priest in the Church of England, had an experience of conversion in 1738. The Methodist movement grew very fast in the British Isles through his itinerant preaching during the eighteenth century, and through Wesley's 'missionaries' it also spread extensively in America.

Pentecostal: Pentecostalism is a fast-growing element in modern Christianity, especially in Latin America, taking its name from the Day of Pentecost when the Holy Spirit was poured out on the apostles. There are several Pentecostal denominations, the largest probably being the Assemblies of God, formed in the USA in 1914.

Moravian: This church came into being in Bohemia in the early eighteenth century, following Lutheran beliefs but with a particular concern to evangelize those as yet unreached by the Christian message. They founded missions in the West Indies, Greenland, South Africa and Labrador. Today the Moravian Church is made up of nineteen self-governing provinces.

When West Meets East
CHRISTIANITY AND THE EASTERN FAITHS

In the long history of the human search for God, Christianity came late on the scene. It grew from the fertile soil of Judaism, the religion of the people of Israel. That faith looks back to its founding father, Abraham, who according to the Bible followed the prompting of God and journeyed east from his homeland to Canaan, perhaps around 2000 BCE. However, by then Hinduism – the main religion of India – was already well established, probably emerging five thousand years ago. Buddhism, following the teaching and spiritual enlightenment of the Buddha, became a reform movement in Hinduism in the fifth century BCE and spread across South-east Asia, China and Japan.

When Jesus began his public ministry, therefore, it was in the context of a deeply religious world, though much of it was quite remote from the experience of the Jews or their Roman conquerors. The seventh century CE saw the emergence of a further highly influential religion, with the teachings of the prophet Muhammad capturing the minds and hearts of much of the Arab world. The five great world faiths had come into being: Hinduism, Judaism, Buddhism, Christianity and Islam. They are with us still.

THE WORLD FAITHS

Hinduism
Emerging probably three millennia before the birth of Jesus, Hinduism is a religious and social system of loosely related sects subscribing to the sacredness of the Veda scriptures. The oldest of these, the Rig-Veda, includes about a thousand hymns of praise to the gods, each of whom, in Hindu thought, represents aspects of the ultimate reality of God. In Hindu thought ultimate reality can only be discovered by direct intuition – by meditation and revelation.

A woman prays over lighted candles at a Hindu temple, Bangalore, India.

Jewish worshippers gather round a Torah scroll at the Western Wall, Jerusalem, during the Feast of Succoth.

Judaism
This is the faith and practice of the Jewish people, technically from the time of the Babylonian exile (sixth century bce), but generally spoken of as from the time of the patriarchs many centuries earlier. When Jews scattered to other lands following the destruction of the Temple in Jerusalem in 70 ce, Judaism became a 'synagogue' religion, the synagogue being where Jews meet to hear the Scriptures, pray and sing psalms and canticles.

Confucianism
This is the ancient religion of China, dating back to the fifth century BCE. Confucius taught that society should be built on principles of absolute justice and moderation. These concepts, allied to a strong sense of traditional values, became the state religion until the Communist revolution.

Christianity and the Other Faiths
● ● ● ● ● ● ● ● ● ● ● ● ● ● ● ● ● ●

The last century has seen many attempts to discover common ground among the major world faiths, including the foundation of a 'World Congress of Faiths'. Sometimes inter-faith 'acts of worship' have taken place, and most of the major Christian churches have entered into dialogue with leaders of the other religions. This has been most effective in the area of Jewish – Christian relationships, but also in the 'Three Faiths Forum', which brings together Christian, Jewish and Islamic leaders.

Where the Eastern religions are concerned there have been fewer formal connections, but with the modern emphasis on 'spirituality' many Christians have begun to investigate what Hinduism and Buddhism have to offer in that area. Since the Beatles' involvement with Eastern spirituality in the 1960s this interest has grown.

Buddhism
Buddhists are the followers of Gautama Buddha (563–483 BCE). His name means 'the enlightened one', and his teaching sought to provide a path to spiritual enlightenment. That path involves right belief, resolve, speech, conduct, occupation, effort, contemplation and meditation. Its final goal is 'Nirvana', the end of all desires and passions. Reincarnation (rebirth in another bodily form) is a crucial element in this path to perfection, but it ceases when one reaches Nirvana. The movement arose within Hinduism, but was in some ways a reaction against its formalism.

Shinto
This is the ancient religion of Japan, incorporating the worship of ancestors and native spirits. It was modified by the influence of Buddhism and Confucianism, but for a while in the 1920s and 1930s it was a state religion in Japan, affording the emperor divine status. Emperor Hirohito disavowed this concept in 1946.

Islam
Islam (the name means 'submission') is a faith that grew from both Jewish and Christian roots. It began and first flourished in Arabic

The Temple of the Dawn is a Buddhist temple on the bank of the Chao Phraya River, Bangkok, Thailand.

soil, through the teachings of Muhammad (570–632 CE), often simply referred to as the Prophet. The Islamic scripture is the Qur'an, written by Muhammad but 'dictated', it is claimed, by the angel Gabriel. For Muslims the Qur'an is the final revelation of truth: there is one God (*Allah* is the Arabic for God), and Muhammad is his Prophet.

Sikhism
This religious movement emerged in the fifteenth century, at about the same time as the Protestant Reformation, offering a simpler and more scripture-based faith than the Hinduism from which it evolved. Its first Guru, Nanak, taught the essential unity of all religions and saw the movement as a potential bridge between Hindus and Muslims. The founding teachers of the Sikh faith, known as the Ten Gurus (the word means 'grave' or 'weighty'), established its fundamental core of belief.

BEDE GRIFFITHS
Bede Griffiths (1906–93) was a Benedictine monk who moved to India, hoping to build a monastery there. Instead, attracted by certain aspects of the Hindu faith, he joined Shantivanam ('Forest of Peace'), an *ashram* – a Hindu religious community. He remained a Catholic priest, but adopted many of the practices of Hindu monastic life and wrote several important books on Hindu–Christian dialogue.

Christianity and Islam

Christianity and Islam are by far the world's largest religions in terms of active followers. By and large Islam holds sway in the Arabic nations, in Pakistan and Afghanistan, in Indonesia and Malaysia, and in parts of Central and North Africa. Christianity is still the dominant cultural and religious influence in the Americas, in most of Europe, in Russia, in sub-Saharan Africa and Australasia, together with a significant minority presence in almost every country in the world. In many of these places Christianity and Islam exist side by side in peace and mutual respect, but any attempt by Christians to win converts from Islam is regarded as unacceptable, and Christians are similarly unhappy about Islamic incursions into traditional Christian 'territory'.

Both religions face the same problem. They do not see their faith in 'comparative' terms: Jesus Christ and Muhammad both claimed to be offering a unique way to God. Given that, how is it possible to accommodate two competing religions, each claiming to be the one way of salvation? Can they finally live alongside each other, or is the question simply, 'Which one will win?'

The al-Haram Mosque complex at Mecca, Saudi Arabia. Every Muslim must try to make the pilgrimage to Mecca at least once in his life.

Francis of Assisi meeting with the Sultan of Egypt, painted by Fra Angelico.

FRANCIS OF ASSISI

In 1219 Francis of Assisi visited Egypt and made contact with Muslim clerics. On his return, he invited several leading Muslims to join him in meeting the Pope in Rome. Francis hoped that a dialogue of minds might lead to a better relationship between the two faiths. However, although the meeting seems to have been friendly, nothing came of it, and the second and subsequent Crusades – wars between Christians and Muslims over the holy sites in Palestine – put an end to hope of a peaceful relationship between Christianity and Islam for many centuries.

What Divides Christians and Muslims

■ While Muslims speak of Jews, Christians and themselves as being 'the people of the Book', sharing faith in one God, they are also clear that the revelation to Muhammad recorded in the Qur'an is the full, final and true message of God to the human race.

■ They do not believe that Jesus died on the cross, but that he was miraculously taken into heaven when the Jews tried to kill him.

■ The Qur'an hotly contests any suggestion that Jesus shared in any way the nature of God. That would be blasphemy.

■ Christians do not see many of their core beliefs reflected in Muslim thought. Although Islam employs the word 'grace' in speaking of God, Muslims do not understand it, as Christians do, as referring to an 'unearned gift'.

■ Muslims reject the idea that Jesus died on the cross for the forgiveness of sins.

■ While they do believe in him as Messiah, Muslims find the notion that Jesus in some way shared the divine nature as blasphemous.

Friday prayers in Suleymanie Mosque, Istanbul, Turkey.

What Christians and Muslims Have in Common

■ Abraham is the common father of Jews, Christians and Muslims. Jews trace their ancestry directly back to him. Muslims trace theirs back to him through his son Ishmael. Christians are children of Abraham because they share his faith in the one God (Romans 4:16).

■ The Qur'an often draws on Old Testament stories and concepts. Christians, of course, accept the Hebrew Scriptures as part of the Bible.

■ Muslims respect and honour Jesus, born of the Virgin Mary, as the Messiah sent by God who healed the sick and even raised the dead. He is the 'Beloved Prophet', who will come again to destroy the anti-Christ. Christians would, of course, want to go much further, but all of this they would accept as true.

■ Both faiths have a firm and deep belief in God.

Important Words and Their Meaning

Muslim: One who 'submits' to God.

Allah: The Arabic word for 'God'.

Imam: The leader of prayers in the mosque.

Jihad: Religious wars of Muslims against unbelievers, but also fighting evil in one's personal life.

Qur'an (Koran): Sacred Arabic text of Islam. Uthman (Caliph from 644 to 56) copied the official version, giving preference to the one originally given in the dialect of Muhammad's tribe. All other versions were destroyed.

Caliph: Formerly head of the Islamic community, but the caliphate finally disappeared in 1924.

Shariah: Islamic law, based on the Qur'an.

Sunni: Followers of the majority group in Islam.

Shi'ites: Followers of the Shi'a sect, which broke away from the Sunnis in 661 CE over the issue of leadership following Muhammad's death.

Salah: The required prayer offered five times a day.

The Independent Spirits
THE PILGRIM FATHERS

The Reformation in England had left the country with a church that was, in the view of some people, either not reformed enough or not Catholic enough. Most people after the accession of Queen Elizabeth seem to have been reasonably happy with the compromise, which was the 'Church of England by Law Established'. But there were devout Roman Catholics who felt alienated by the new regime, and were indeed regarded as akin to traitors by some loyalists. On the other side, there were groups of people who felt that the Reformation in England had not gone far enough. What they saw as 'popish practices' continued. Bishops and priests were still in charge of the church. The set order of service, the 'liturgy', had to be meticulously followed. Such people, many of them influenced by the Swiss Reformers, wanted an altogether more independent, congregational, lay-led church.

These people of independent spirit felt stifled by the religious atmosphere of the 'old world' of Europe. They sought freedom to explore and express new ways of following Jesus. Because they talked of a more 'pure' church, they were dubbed 'Puritans', and seemed to accept the title. As they strove to find somewhere to practise their beliefs, unhindered by state religion or national laws, they could never have imagined what momentous consequences their actions would have.

Mayflower II in dock at Plymouth, Massachusetts. It is a replica of the ship that brought the Pilgrims to the New World in 1620.

The Pilgrim Fathers

One group of Puritans met in All Saints' parish church in Babworth, Nottinghamshire, where the parson, Richard Clyfton, held Separatist beliefs very similar to those of the nonconformist or independent movements. This group felt increasingly compromised by their affiliation to the Church of England, which they saw as at best half-reformed. Eventually the whole congregation, including their parson, left the Church of England and began gathering for worship in Scrooby Manor House. One of their number, Brewster, the 'presiding elder', was fined £20 (about £2,000 at current values) for failing to worship in the Church of England. It was events like this, and further harassment and abuse, that led the congregation to decide to move to Amsterdam, to join other Separatists who had already found refuge there.

From Amsterdam to Virginia

It was a difficult and dangerous operation, and in the end they did not find the Netherlands particularly congenial, largely because of difficulties over language, employment and culture. Eventually, seeing it as a missionary operation, they decided to sail as a party to Virginia in America, where one such Puritan settlement had already been established. An initial group of 120 mostly younger men and women set sail in the *Mayflower* in September 1620.

The story of their journey is a thrilling one, and they were able to establish a Puritan colony in Virginia later that year. Americans know them as 'the Pilgrims'; in the UK they are usually called 'the Pilgrim Fathers'.

The Act of Uniformity

In 1549 the English parliament passed the First Act of Uniformity. This, and subsequent legislation over the next few years, was designed to ensure that only the *Book of Common Prayer* was used in public worship, that everyone attended their parish church, and that anyone organizing alternative religious gatherings could be imprisoned. Those who did not conform were 'nonconformists' – on the one hand Roman Catholics, and on the other the so-called 'Separatists'. A century later a further Act of Uniformity sought to restore order after the Puritan 'Commonwealth' of Cromwell. It required all clergy publicly to affirm their assent to the *Book of Common Prayer*, and removed from office all who had not been ordained by a bishop. About two thousand Presbyterian ministers were ejected from their parishes.

OLIVER CROMWELL

Oliver Cromwell was a member of the English parliament but strongly supported the religious and political agenda of the Puritans. When civil war broke out in 1642 he saw it as a religious struggle for the soul of the nation. His army of 'Roundheads' was well trained and efficient and defeated the 'Cavaliers', the royalist forces. The king, Charles I, was executed and Cromwell, having dismissed the parliament, appointed himself 'Lord Protector of the Commonwealth'. Bishops, deans and cathedral chapters were removed, religious ornaments and statues desecrated and the *Book of Common Prayer* banned. Theatres were closed, dancing and feasting discouraged and Christmas celebrations abolished. Public support for Cromwell waned, and after his death the Puritan government fell apart.

Cromwell's troops destroying religious statues and ornaments.

AND A SCEPTICAL FOOTNOTE…

'We are descended from the Puritans, who nobly fled from a land of despotism to a land of freedom, where they could not only enjoy their own religion, but prevent everybody else from enjoying his.'
ARTEMUS WARD

What Became of 'Puritanism'?

Although it is considered incorrect to use the title 'Puritan' of people after 1660, the fact is that Puritan ideas have persisted in all of the non-Roman Catholic churches. The Independents, the Baptists, the Presbyterians and later the Methodists all owed something to that stubborn streak of moral fervour that marked out the Puritans at their best. A strong tradition of Puritan thinking has also influenced some Anglicans in the evangelical tradition.

Probably most significantly of all, the ethos of the Puritan fathers has deeply affected American Christianity. Many churches in the USA see it as part of their mission to stand up for high moral and ethical principles in private and public life.

The Evangelicals
'YOU MUST BE BORN AGAIN'

The media have popularized the phrase 'born-again Christian' to describe those who would more correctly be called 'evangelicals' – after all, according to the Bible, *all* Christians must be 'born again' (see John 3:3). Evangelicals are a major force in modern Christianity, especially in the USA. The word means 'Gospel-based', and the emphasis of their belief and spirituality is on the gospel message of Jesus and the apostles: repentance for sin; belief in Jesus and especially his sacrifice on the cross for the forgiveness of sins; and the presence of the Holy Spirit in the life of the believer.

'Evangelical' is the traditional name of the Lutheran churches in Germany and Switzerland (*Evangelische Kirche*), given to distinguish them from the Calvinist or Reformed churches, but elsewhere it has been confined to Christians and churches that share the distinctive evangelical doctrines. As might be expected, they are committed to evangelism – sharing with as many people as possible the 'good news' (which is what the biblical word 'gospel' means). They have been in the forefront of the missionary movements in Africa, Asia and Latin America.

What Evangelicals Believe

1. The supreme authority and reliability of the Bible.

2 . The orthodox Christian doctrine of God as Father, Son and Holy Spirit, the Creator of all that exists.

3. The justification of the sinner solely on the grounds of God's grace received by faith.

4. The death of Jesus Christ on the cross as a sacrifice for the sins of the world.

5. The necessity of personal conversion and assurance of salvation.

6. The Christian church as a community of believers centred on the word of God.

7. The priesthood of all believers – that is, every Christian has equal access to God and can minister to others on God's behalf.

8. The work of the Holy Spirit in the life of the Christian, producing the 'fruit of the Spirit'.

9. The resurrection of Jesus Christ, and through him the promise of eternal life to those who put their trust in him.

10. The personal return of Jesus Christ in glory to judge the world.

Jonathan Edwards, one of the leading figures of revival in eighteenth-century America.

Revival Movements

Evangelicalism, as distinct from the evangelical message, which is as old as Christianity itself, dates back to the eighteenth century and the ministry of the Wesley brothers and George Whitefield. John and Charles Wesley masterminded what was known as the 'Methodist Revival', which permanently changed the face of church life in the British Isles and far beyond. George Whitefield, an equally striking orator though of more Calvinistic views, saw himself as an 'awakener' to all the churches. In America he helped to stimulate what was called the 'Great Awakening' of the early eighteenth century, alongside Jonathan Edwards.

Properly speaking a 'revival' is a renewal of spiritual life in the churches through the work of the Holy Spirit. Notable revivals have occurred in south Wales, in the Hebrides and in Rwanda in East Africa.

WILLIBALD BEYSCHLAG

Beyschlag (1823–1900) was a major figure in German evangelical theology, helping to draw up the Constitution of the Prussian Church in the nineteenth century. He also founded the *Evangelische Bund* (Evangelical League) in Germany in 1866–87, to defend Protestant interests against what was seen as growing Catholic influence.

EVANGELICALS AND EVANGELISM

Charles Finney (1792–1875) was an outstanding evangelist and preacher in the USA in the first half of the nineteenth century. A Presbyterian minister, he rose to fame as an itinerant revivalist preacher, later abandoning the Presbyterian fold and joining the Congregationalists. It is said that he transformed the revivalist movement in America, employing a dramatic pulpit style, and introduced the idea of 'protracted' meetings that lasted several days, lengthy prayer meetings, and the practice of praying for individuals by name in public. He rejected a Calvinist approach and taught that human beings have the individual responsibility to respond to the gospel message.

Dwight L. Moody (1837–99) (above) was an outstanding evangelist who conducted campaigns across the USA and Britain. He was joined by Ira D. Sankey (above right), whose songs and hymns became a feature of their meetings and were eventually published in the *Sankey and Moody Hymnbook*, widely used in revivalist circles. Moody founded a Bible institute in Chicago.

PEACE WITH GOD

'A great many people are trying to make peace, but that has already been done. God has not left it for us to do; all we have to do is to enter into it.'
DWIGHT L. MOODY

Billy Graham (born 1918) is probably the most distinguished of a long line of American evangelists. A Baptist, he began his campaigns in Los Angeles in 1949 and by the mid-1950s he had become an international figure. His 'crusades', as they were then called, in Britain in 1954, 1955 and 1966 were hugely supported and achieved recognition from across the Christian spectrum. He was a counsellor to several American presidents and travelled widely with his message, even to Communist countries.

'Signs Following'

THE PENTECOSTALISTS

Pentecostalists take their name from the events on the Day of Pentecost described in the New Testament (Acts 2), when the disciples were 'filled with the Spirit' and preached to the crowds in the street. Many didn't speak Aramaic (the language of Jesus and the disciples), yet as Peter and the others began to preach to them they each heard what was said in their own language. At the end of Peter's address he called on them to repent, to be baptized in the name of Jesus and to 'receive the promised Holy Spirit'. According to Acts, three thousand people were baptized that day, and the Christian church was born.

The Pentecostal movement, which is relatively modern, and the churches associated with it, claim to represent this early tradition. They expect their members to exercise the 'gifts of the Spirit', including speaking in tongues. They tend to offer a more spontaneous style of worship and prayer than most of the traditional churches.

THE CHARISMATIC MOVEMENT

This movement, which first achieved prominence in the USA in about 1960, saw many of the beliefs and practices of the Pentecostal churches being adopted by the mainstream denominations. It soon also took root in Britain and the rest of Europe, affecting most of the traditional denominations, and often resulted in failing churches suddenly experiencing huge growth in numbers and enthusiasm. The movement was officially recognized by the Roman Catholic Church at the Synod of Bishops in Rome in 1987.

RENEWAL FROM THE INSIDE

'Spirituality really means "Holy Spirit at work", a profound action of the Holy Spirit in his church, renewing that church from the inside.'
CARDINAL LEON SUENENS

The Descent of the Holy Spirit. Fifteenth-century Russian icon from the Cathedral of St Sophia, Novgorod.

● SEE ALSO
THE HOLY SPIRIT P24-25

Pentecostal Churches

The modern Pentecostal movement had its beginnings in various revivalist churches in the USA, first coming to prominence in Los Angeles in 1906. As the movement grew, many of the groups formed what was and is the largest Pentecostal denomination, the Assemblies of God, in 1914.

The movement spread to Britain in 1907 and from there to Europe – including the Soviet Union, as it then was, where Pentecostalists were viewed with suspicion by the Communist authorities. Immigration to Britain from the Caribbean introduced black-led churches of Pentecostal style to Europe, including the New Testament Church of God.

In the last decades of the twentieth century Pentecostalism began to flourish in Latin America, where it made big inroads into previously Catholic areas. Brazil, for instance, has 15 million Pentecostal Christians.

ALPHA

One highly successful off-shoot of the charismatic movement has been 'Alpha', an introductory course in Christian belief launched by Holy Trinity Church, Brompton, London. Widely advertised on buses, stations, hoardings and on television, it has drawn several million people in Europe, the USA and elsewhere to take part in informal suppers followed by open-ended discussion about issues of faith. Although the content of the course itself is 'mainstream' Christian, the teaching on the Holy Spirit and on spiritual gifts is clearly charismatic.

Key Beliefs

1. 'Baptism in the Holy Spirit', which Pentecostals see as a separate and distinct event from baptism in water, whereby the believer receives one or more of the 'gifts of the Spirit'.

2. The exercise of the gifts of the Spirit, especially speaking in tongues (another language), interpreting tongues, prophecy, exorcism and spiritual healing.

3. The use of these gifts in public worship as well as private devotion.

4. Spontaneous and extempore worship.

In other respects, Pentecostal churches hold orthodox Christian beliefs about God, Jesus, the Holy Spirit and salvation, and observe the ordinances of baptism and the Lord's Supper.

SECRETS OF SUCCESS

'The phenomenal growth of Pentecostalism has been due in large part to the enthusiastic vitality of their experience of the Holy Spirit, their spontaneous style of worship in which all can participate in their own way, the absence of a caste of clergy and of a priestly hierarchy, and of the insistence that all members must share their faith with others.'
JAMES D. G. DUNN

A healing service in progress at Peniel Pentecostal Church, Brentcross, England.

Beyond the Fringe
SECTS AND HERESIES

There have always been breakaway groups in the church, and sects that deviate from orthodox Christian teaching – usually about the nature of Christ or belief in the Trinity. However, the last two hundred years have seen a proliferation of them, with the main emphasis of many such groups now being the 'End Times' – the Second Coming of Jesus and events associated with it. Some of these sects are very large numerically: the Jehovah's Witnesses, for example, have about six million members world-wide.

Some of the sects retain a good deal of standard Christian teaching, simply adding their own distinctive, but a fairly common factor is a rejection of the divine nature of Jesus (the 'Son of God'). Most of them are highly critical of what we might call 'established' Christianity and the traditional churches. The majority of them have their origins in the USA, mostly in the nineteenth century, when interest in prophecy was allied to a fierce independence of spirit. Many were lay-led movements, which appealed to that same spirit. Some have disappeared, but there are always new ones ready to replace them.

SOME MODERN SECTS

Jehovah's Witnesses:
Founded in 1881 by a Pennsylvanian draper and former Congregationalist, C. T. Russell. He believed that Jesus Christ had returned invisibly to earth in 1874 to prepare for the kingdom of God, which would materialize in 1914. As well as these Adventist views, Russell rejected many orthodox Christian doctrines, including the divinity of Christ. His successor as leader was J. F. Rutherford, who led the movement into theocracy (government by God alone), which resulted in Witnesses in many countries clashing with governments. They are best known for their door-to-door missionary work, for their paper *The Watchtower*, and for their refusal to accept blood transfusions.

Christian Science:
In 1874 Mary Baker Eddy wrote two books: *Science and Health* and *Key to the Scriptures.* These became the foundation documents of the Church of Christ Scientist, which was founded in Boston, Massachussets, in 1879. Christian Scientists believe that anything that does not express the nature of God is 'unreal', and that includes sickness and evil. They can be overcome by the believer's trust in God's power and love, rather than by medical treatment. The movement publishes a highly respected international newspaper, the *Christian Science Monitor*.

WHAT IS 'HERESY'?

The word 'heresy' is seldom used in church circles nowadays, but until modern times it was applied to those who wilfully rejected a belief that was essential to the catholic (that is, world-wide) faith. The root of the word is the Greek word for 'choice', and heresy implies that the heretic has *chosen* to believe something contrary to received Christian truth. Until the end of the sixteenth century heretics were frequently put to death by the church authorities, 'for the good of their souls'.

THE HERETIC

'The heretic is not a man who loves truth too much; no one can love truth too much. The heretic is the man who loves his truth more than truth itself. He prefers the half-truth he has found to the whole truth which humanity has found.'

G. K. CHESTERTON

● SEE ALSO
CHRISTIANITY P8-9
THE CROSS P18-19

The Mormons: Full name, Church of Jesus Christ of Latter-Day Saints. Founded in Manchester, New York, in 1830 by Joseph Smith, it offers a version of Christianity for the New World. Smith claimed to have discovered some gold plates in a cave, which he was able to interpret by wearing special glasses provided by an angel. The plates provided the text for the *Book of Mormon*, which his followers regard as on a par with the Bible. Mormons believe that Jesus ministered briefly in America after his resurrection and that the New Jerusalem will be built in the Western hemisphere. Since 1847 their headquarters have been located in Salt Lake City, Utah. The movement gave up its practice of polygamy – advocated by Smith – in 1890, under government pressure. The Mormons claim some eleven million members world-wide.

The Mormon temple at La Jolla, San Diego, California.

Christadelphians: Founded in America in 1848 by John Thomas, they believe that Jesus Christ will return in power to set up a theocracy (direct government by God) in Jerusalem. They hold that this belief is essential to salvation.

Spiritualism: People have always sought to communicate with the dead, a practice roundly condemned in the Bible (Leviticus 19:31). In its modern form, Spiritualism dates from the occult experiences of the Fox family in America in 1848. It usually includes the use of a medium and involves a 'seance', a meeting at which people attempt to make contact with the dead. There are Christian Spiritualist churches, which profess to follow the leadership of Jesus Christ, but their beliefs differ widely from those of the mainstream churches, especially about the role and nature of Jesus.

Spiritualists join hands around a ouija board.

After the Squabbles and the Splits
PUTTING THE PIECES TOGETHER AGAIN

The 'ecumenical movement' – literally the 'world-wide movement' – is the name that has been given to the efforts of the world's Christian churches to repair the damage done by centuries of squabbles, splits, schisms and walk-outs. From the time of the apostles there have been divisions in the church, usually over matters of belief, but also over questions of authority. The first major split, as we have seen, took place in the eleventh century, when the Eastern church split from the West, principally over the question of the supremacy of the Pope. Four centuries later the Protestant Reformation saw a further huge split in the church, but this time the split itself gave rise to further splits, so that there are now literally thousands of Protestant denominations across the world. Two centuries after the Reformation, the Wesleyan Revival saw another split – that of the 'Methodists' from the Church of England.

It wasn't until the early twentieth century that all of this was fully recognized as an appalling scandal and a complete denial of the prayer of Jesus that his followers would be 'one' (John 17:21). At the Edinburgh Conference of 1910, church leaders from many Protestant churches pledged themselves to take to heart the problem of Christian disunity, and in that decision the modern ecumenical movement was born.

Later, in the 1960s, the Orthodox churches began to be closely involved in the ecumenical movement, including the World Council of Churches, and after the Second Vatican Council the Roman Catholic Church initiated a number of moves aimed at improving relationships with the Orthodox and many other churches. It appointed 'observers' to the World Council of Churches.

Steps Towards Unity

1910 The Edinburgh Conference – mainly Western Protestant church leaders. This led to:

1921 International Missionary Council, to coordinate the work of mission agencies around the world. This led to:

1925 Establishment of the Universal Christian Conference on Life and Work, which led to:

1927 First World Conference on Faith and Order, in Lausanne, Switzerland. From this point, some Eastern Orthodox and Oriental Orthodox churches became interested, which led to:

1948 Formation of the World Council of Churches, which included Orthodox as well as Protestant and Anglican churches.

1961 For the first time, Roman Catholic observers attended the Third Assembly of the WCC.

1962–65 The Second Vatican Council, called by Pope John XXIII and completed under his successor, Pope Paul VI, had as one of its ultimate goals the unity of all Christians. Extensive reforms were brought in, including the general replacement of Latin as the language of worship. Dialogues were subsequently established with the Orthodox, Lutheran, Anglican and Methodist Churches.

UNITING CHURCHES

■ In 1925 the United Church of Canada was formed by bringing together Methodist, Congregationalist and most Presbyterian churches. This United Church is the second largest church in Canada, behind the Roman Catholics.

■ In 1947 the Church of South India was inaugurated. It was a union of three existing churches: the South India United Church (an earlier union of Presbyterian, Congregational and Dutch Reformed churches); the Anglican Church of India, Burma and Ceylon (Sri Lanka); and the Methodist Church of South India.

■ In 1970 the Church of North India was formed by the union of six bodies: Anglicans, Congregationalists, Presbyterians, Baptists, Disciples of Christ and some Methodists. It is in full communion with the Church of England.

■ In 1972 the United Reformed Church was formed by the union of most Congregational churches in England and Wales with the Presbyterian Church of England. In 1981 most of the Churches of Christ in Britain joined it, but as some of them were in Scotland its name was changed to the United Reformed Church in the United Kingdom. In fact, the Congregational Union in Scotland also joined in 2000.

In most of these union schemes there were churches that 'opted out', thus creating in some cases yet another denomination.

Pope Paul VI seated on the papal throne on the steps of St Peter's Basilica, Rome, during the opening ceremonial mass of the Second Vatican Council, 1962.

AN ECUMENICAL 'CREED'

In things essential, Unity.
In things indifferent, Generosity.
In all things, Charity.

What People Have Said About Unity

● ● ● ● ● ● ● ● ● ● ● ● ● ● ● ● ● ●

Behold how good and pleasant it is for brethren to dwell together in unity!
PSALM 133:1

'Form all together one choir, so that with the symphony of your feelings, and having all taken the tone of God, you may sing with one voice to the Father through Jesus Christ.'
IGNATIUS OF ANTIOCH

'Church unity is like peace. We are all for it, but we are not willing to pay the price.'
VISSER'T HOOFT

'Our divisions prevent the neighbours from hearing the gospel as they should.'
POPE JOHN PAUL II

'Some of us worked long enough in a shipbuilding district to know that welding is impossible except the materials to be joined are at white heat. When you try to weld them, they fall apart.'
GEORGE F. MACLEOD

WEEK OF PRAYER FOR CHRISTIAN UNITY

Since 1908 a group of high church Anglicans had begun to observe the week of 18–25 January as an Octave of Prayer for Church Unity – specifically, in their case, reunion

with the Roman Catholic Church. Later, and largely through the work of a French priest, Paul Couturier, this developed into a more general Week of Prayer for Christian Unity, which is widely observed all over the world.

'I ask not only on behalf of these, but also on behalf of those who will believe in me through their word, that they may all be one. As you, Father, are in me and I am in you, may they also be in us, so that the world may believe that you have sent me.'
JESUS IN JOHN 17:20, 21

PAUL COUTURIER

Couturier was a French priest who was greatly influenced by the Benedictine monks at Amay-sur-Meuse and later at Chevetogne in Belgium. They had been asked by Pope Pius XI to pray for Christian unity, and sought to restore closer relations between the Roman Catholic and other churches. While staying with them, Couturier's interest in the emerging ecumenical movement was aroused. He adapted the Octave of Prayer for Unity to a wider cause, embracing the unity of the whole of Christendom. Taken up by both the Catholic leadership and the World Council of Churches, it still flourishes today, though the earnest prayers offered every year have so far produced no more than a general improvement in warmth and mutual respect between the different churches. Couturier worked tirelessly in the cause of unity until his death in 1953, corresponding widely and writing many tracts and pamphlets on the subject.

The Nativity
THE MANGER AND THE BABY

Christmas is one of the three great festivals of Christianity. It celebrates the birth of Jesus Christ, though no one would claim that it is observed on his actual birthday – there is no record of that. Christians belonging to the churches in the Western tradition started observing Christmas on 25 December from the early fourth century, probably to counter a festival of the sun, which had been a popular mid-winter festival in the Roman empire. The Eastern church at first tended to emphasize the Epiphany (the visit of the 'Wise Men' to the child Jesus) on 6 January, but eventually 25 December was generally adopted as the feast of the Nativity.

The actual birth of Jesus occurred, according to the Gospels, during the reign of Herod the Great, who died in 4 BCE, which suggests that the traditional dating of the 'year of Our Lord' is slightly adrift – and that the millennium was celebrated at least four years too late! The birthplace of Jesus in Bethlehem became a place of pilgrimage from the early fourth century, when Constantine built a church on the probable site.

THE MANGER

'This will be a sign for you,' the angel told the shepherds. 'You will find the child wrapped in cloths and lying in a manger.' The 'child' was a 'Saviour, who is the Messiah, the Lord', yet they would identify him as they searched Bethlehem by the lowliest of all settings – he would be lying in a feeding trough.

People in the Christmas Story

Mary: A young woman, probably no more than 14 years old, who was 'betrothed' (engaged) to be married to the village carpenter, Joseph. She had been told in a vision that she would bear a child who would be called 'the Son of the Most High' (Luke 1:32).

Joseph: The village carpenter in Nazareth, who was engaged to be married to a young girl called Mary. When she told him that she was pregnant he planned to end the engagement quietly, to avoid scandal, until he was told in a dream–vision that the child to be born was 'from the Holy Spirit' (Matthew 1:20). Joseph, who was probably much older than Mary, had evidently died before Jesus began his public ministry 30 years later.

The Adoration of the Magi by the fifteenth-century Spanish artist, Jaime Ferrer.

The Wise Men: Or more correctly the 'Magi'. As that name suggests, they were skilled in the 'magic' arts – soothsayers, astrologers, fortune-tellers. The ancient world was profoundly influenced by such people: no king would go to war, no merchant would strike a deal, unless the 'signs' were propitious. The early church saw the Magi as representatives of the old order of superstition and fear, and drew comfort from the notion that they fell down before the infant Christ and worshipped him.

Herod the Great: Ruled the land of Judea as a Roman puppet from 37 to 4 BCE. He began the restoration of the Temple in Jerusalem, extending it to a massive size (it occupied a quarter of the city). He was a cruel and ruthless king who murdered his own wife and two sons, so the story of the slaughter of baby boys in Bethlehem would not have been out of character if he saw one of them as a rival to his authority. There is, however, no mention of this massacre in the history of the period by the Jewish writer Josephus.

BETHLEHEM

In the days of Herod, Bethlehem was a small town about 5 miles (8 km) from Jerusalem, but it had a special place in Jewish history as the birthplace of the great King David. The prophet Micah foretold that one day there would come from Bethlehem a new ruler for Israel, who would restore its former glory (Micah 5:2). Both Gospel records of the birth of Jesus (in Matthew and Luke) place his birth in Bethlehem and see it as fulfilling Micah's prophecy.

SHEPHERDS

'While shepherds watched their flocks by night', the carol says, 'an angel of the Lord came down and glory shone around.' That's how Luke introduces his story of the birth of Jesus, the shepherds being the first people to be told of the event. Leaving their flocks, they hurried down from the surrounding hills to find the child 'lying in a manger'. The story makes two important connections. The obvious one is to David, who was himself a young shepherd boy when he was anointed as the future king of Israel. The second is to Luke's constant concern to show that Jesus came especially for the marginalized, despised and poor, shepherds being by the nature of their trade unable to fulfil the usual requirements of religious Jews.

The Shepherds' Fields at Beth Sahur, near Bethlehem.

What People Have Said About Christmas

'The Word of God became man that you also may learn from a man how a man becomes a God.'
CLEMENT OF ALEXANDRIA

'The greatness of God was not put off, but the slightness of human nature was put on.'
THOMAS AQUINAS

'It is good to be children sometimes, and never better than at Christmas, when its mighty Founder became a child himself.'
CHARLES DICKENS

'The fact of Jesus' coming is the final and unanswerable proof that God cares.'
WILLIAM BARCLAY

'The simple shepherds heard the voice of an angel and found their Lamb. The wise men saw a star and found their Wisdom.'
FULTON J. SHEEN

Christmas in Church

The observance of Christmas varies a good deal according to local tradition and denominational preferences, but the following are some of the most common features of the celebration of the festival in church:

The Crib: Popularized by Francis of Assisi, the 'crib', a model of the supposed scene in the stable where Jesus was born, is a feature of Christmas in many churches. Central to the crib, with its figures of Mary, Joseph and the shepherds, is the manger holding the baby Jesus. The 'Blessing of the Crib' is a service often performed on Christmas Eve.

Midnight Mass: A service of Holy Communion that reaches its climax at about midnight is now a strong feature of Christmas observance in most churches. In Roman Catholic churches Christmas is often marked by three Masses: one at midnight, one at dawn, and one during the day.

Carols: From the Middle Ages onwards simple 'carols' – songs celebrating various aspects of the birth of Jesus – have been part of Christmas worship. There is a strong tradition of such carols in most European countries, and many of them have been successfully translated into other languages. Among the best known are '*Stille Nacht*' ('Silent night'), '*Adeste Fideles*' ('O come all ye faithful'), 'Hark the herald angels sing' and the traditional Czech carol 'Little Jesus, sweetly sleep'.

ST NICHOLAS

The practice of giving presents to children at Christmas probably stems from the story of Nicholas, who was bishop of Myra (in modern Turkey) in the fourth century. Among many of his charitable activities, it seems that he gave presents to poor children at Christmas to mark the Saviour's birthday. In the Lowlands this practice took place on the feast of St Nicholas (6 December) and was carried to America by Dutch settlers. 'Santa Claus' is simply a corruption of his name – Saint Nicholas, or, in Dutch, Sinter Klaus.

The traditional robes of Santa Claus ('Father Christmas') are based on those of a bishop, the red cloak being his cope and the hat his mitre.

The Empty Tomb
CELEBRATING EASTER

Easter is the most important festival of the Christian year because it celebrates the most significant event in the story of Jesus, his resurrection from the dead. The apostle Paul said that if Christ had not risen, the faith of Christians would be 'in vain' and 'futile' (1 Corinthians 15:14, 17). Unlike the followers of the other great world faiths, Christians do not simply follow the teachings or example of a great leader who is now dead, but of a Saviour whom they believe to be fully alive.

So Easter is crucial to the whole case for Christianity. If Jesus died and stayed dead, then the heart of Christianity has been removed. But if God raised him from the dead, as Christians believe, then our whole understanding of the meaning of life and the inevitability of death is transformed. Christianity, in other words, is an Easter faith, or it is nothing.

WHO MOVED THE STONE?

Influenced by rationalist thought at the end of the nineteenth century, a lawyer called Frank Morison decided to take three years away from his practice to disprove the resurrection of Jesus. However, at the end of those three years he concluded that the weight of evidence strongly supported the truth of the resurrection of Jesus, and he wrote a book, *Who Moved the Stone?*, which has become a religious classic, still in print over a century later.

DATING EASTER

The dating of Easter has been a matter of dispute almost throughout Christian history. Today, despite both East and West following the Gregorian calendar, the method of dating means that sometimes the Eastern and Western churches celebrate Easter on the same date, but sometimes the Orthodox Easter can fall as many as five weeks later than the Western one. The date is determined by the timing of the spring equinox.

The Easter Story
. . . .

Doubting Thomas by Rembrandt van Rijn, 1634.

All four Gospels relate the story of the resurrection of Jesus, and their accounts are supported by the earliest record we have, which is in Paul's first letter to the church at Corinth. He reminds them of what he preached to them, a message based on what he himself had been taught when he was baptized. Christ 'died for our sins', he was 'buried', and on the third day he was 'raised' and appeared to Peter and the other apostles and subsequently to many other disciples – 'more than five hundred', he claimed – 'most of whom are still alive'. He wrote this in about 55 CE, just over twenty years after the crucifixion of Jesus.

The Gospels tell the story in more detail, though those details vary to some extent, and even appear occasionally to contradict each other over minor matters (how and when the body of Jesus was anointed, for example). So this was not a matter of collusion to present a convincing story (or they would have got the details right!), nor could it have been self-delusion or hallucination on a grand scale, because too many people were involved. The Gospel writers struggle to find words to describe their experience of the risen Jesus, but through it all there is an unshakeable conviction that they were witnesses of something utterly unique but totally convincing.

FOUR ACCOUNTS OF THE RESURRECTION OF JESUS

Matthew
Mary Magdalene and 'the other Mary' visit the tomb. Angel rolled stone away – guards fled. Angel: 'He has been raised.' Women tell the others. Jesus appears to the eleven in Galilee.

Mark
Mary Magdalene and two other women visit the tomb. Stone had been rolled back. Tomb empty. A 'young man' says, 'He is not here. He has been raised. Tell the disciples, and Peter.'

Luke
Mary Magdalene and two other women come to the tomb. Stone rolled away, tomb empty. Peter runs to the tomb and 'sees' the graveclothes. Risen Jesus appears to disciples at Emmaus and in the Upper Room.

John
Mary Magdalene comes to the tomb. Stone rolled away, tomb empty. Peter and John run to the tomb, see and 'believe'. Jesus appears to Mary Magdalene and to various disciples in Jerusalem and Galilee.

From this chart we can draw out the common elements of all the Gospel accounts.

1. Mary Magdalene was the first to the tomb (with other women).

2. The stone had been rolled back.

3. The tomb was empty.

4. Jesus appeared to various disciples in Jerusalem and Galilee.

JOHN MORRIS

'The truth of the resurrection is like a big tree: we can cut off a few branches that we think are mere legends, but the central stem or trunk remains strong... Why the tree grew at all demands explanation: critics have offered interesting alternative theories, but I have not been sufficiently persuaded to demolish the tree.'
CONTEMPORARY CREED

Celebrating Easter

In the early church those who were being prepared for baptism (the 'catechumens') spent the whole of the night of Easter Eve in prayer and were baptized very early on Easter morning. Later these ceremonies were put back to the Saturday, but since 1951 they have been restored in the Roman Catholic Church to the night of Saturday–Sunday (the 'Easter Vigil'). Many other churches mark Easter in a similar way, or with a sunrise service, and some follow the Roman Catholic practice of lighting the Paschal Candle and carrying it in procession into the church, symbolizing the new life of Easter.

The Orthodox churches follow the ancient tradition of a Eucharist and baptisms on Saturday, with the Mattins of Easter Sunday at midnight, followed by the liturgy of Easter Day. In Orthodox countries the rest of the day is for public celebration.

A Catholic priest lights a Paschal (Easter) Candle inside the Church of the Nativity in Bethlehem at the start of the Easter Vigil.

MARY MAGDALENE

Obviously Mary Magdalene was an important element in the story of the resurrection of Jesus. The authenticity of the Gospel accounts is strengthened by this fact, because in contemporary Jewish thought women were not reliable witnesses, and that would be especially true of a woman like her who had a record of emotional or moral problems (see Luke 8:2). Yet she is the undisputed first witness of the resurrection in every single account.

The meeting of the risen Christ with Mary Magdalene, painted by Titian in 1514.

C. S. LEWIS

'I believe in the resurrection in the same way as I believe in the sunrise: because I see it, but more because by it I see everything else.'

Pentecost
THE HEAVENLY HELPER

The third great festival of Christianity, alongside Christmas and Easter, is Pentecost, or 'Whitsun', as it used to be called. This day recalls the gift of the promised Holy Spirit to the disciples, the first public preaching of the resurrection of Jesus, and the conversion (Luke claims, in Acts) of three thousand people, who were baptized by the apostles. For these reasons it is often called 'the birthday of the church'.

Although Pentecost is a major Christian festival, it has never acquired in the West the same public attention as Christmas, or to a lesser extent Easter.

'Pentecost' is the Greek name for the Jewish Feast of Weeks, which falls on the fiftieth day after the Passover. The Christian festival of Pentecost is celebrated therefore on the seventh Sunday after Easter, ten days after the Feast of the Ascension. For Christians, it is taken as a reminder that the faith is not simply a matter of intellectual assent ('I believe the Creed') or moral discipline ('I try to keep the Law of God'), but of an openness to the Spirit of God working in human lives and in the world. Without that Spirit, human effort is fruitless, human worship empty and meaningless, and our churches barren shrines.

From Easter to Pentecost

After Jesus appeared to the disciples on the third day after his crucifixion, the Gospels record many more appearances to them, not only in the Upper Room where they were hiding from the authorities, but also on a walk to Emmaus and at Lake Galilee. However, after 40 days he met them on a hillside – unnamed, but traditionally assumed to be the Mount of Olives – and was 'taken up out of their sight' in a cloud (Acts 1:1–9). On this occasion he promised them that though he was leaving them they would be 'endued with power from on high' if they waited in Jerusalem, and would then be his 'witnesses' to the whole world. Ten days later, on the Day of Pentecost, that promise was fulfilled, and the first public witness was made to the resurrection of Jesus. The Ascension is marked by the church on the fortieth day after Easter, a Thursday, and observed as a national holiday in many Christian countries.

The Ascension of Christ, fresco by Giotto in the Scrovegni Chapel, Padua, Italy.

One of the last mass pilgrimages in Europe, the Romeria del Rocio, is travelled from Sevilla to Almonte, a village 50 miles (80 km) away from Sevilla. The pilgrimage lasts four days and a million pilgrims walk the Rocio path to celebrate Pentecost.

Young girls wear white robes and hoods at a Pentecost Monday service of confirmation at Chartres Cathedral, France.

What People Have Said About the Holy Spirit
••••••••••••••••••••

'Those who have the gale of the Holy Spirit go forward even in sleep.'
BROTHER LAWRENCE

'Every time we say "I believe in the Holy Spirit", we mean that we believe there is a living God able and willing to enter human personality and change it.'
J. B. PHILLIPS

'I should as soon attempt to raise flowers if there were no atmosphere, or produce fruits if there were neither light nor heat, as to regenerate men if I did not believe there was a Holy Spirit.'
HENRY WARD BEECHER

Vigil of Pentecost
••••••••••••••••••

In the Western church the Vigil of Pentecost became from early days a secondary date for baptisms, possibly because of the 'mass baptism' on the original Day of Pentecost in Jerusalem. The service resembled the Paschal (Easter) Vigil in form. In the Orthodox churches the feast is observed in honour of the Holy Trinity, with the following Monday being dedicated to celebrate the Holy Spirit.

Many churches across the world now mark Pentecost as a festival of joy and spiritual power, with processions, music and open air services. For churches in the Pentecostal and charismatic traditions it is an important opportunity to mark the event that saw the outpouring of the Spirit upon the church.

WHITSUNDAY

Pentecost was known in English as Whitsunday because of the white robes or dresses worn by candidates for baptism – Whitsun being, with Easter, the great season for baptisms. In towns in northern England, especially, it was known for the 'Whit Walks', when children from the churches paraded through the streets with banners and flowers.

Belonging
THE 'BADGE' THAT CHRISTIANS WEAR

There are two elements to being a Christian. One is believing in Jesus Christ; the other is belonging to his community, the church. The 'badge' or sign marking someone who both believes and belongs is baptism. In Christian terminology it is a 'sacrament', an outward sign of something that is happening inwardly – in this case, faith.

Baptism was practised among the Jewish people before the lifetime of Jesus. The word simply means 'washing' or 'cleansing', and was usually a ritual in which water was poured on someone or they were dipped in it (in a river, for instance). John the Baptist, who foretold the coming of Jesus, called people to a baptism of 'repentance' – it was a sign of sorrow for past sins and a determination to make a fresh start.

Jesus told his disciples to baptize those who would believe in him through their teaching. This 'baptism' was to mark a death to their old life and a birth to a new one of faith in him within the community of the church.

Following these instructions, on the Day of Pentecost the apostles baptized about three thousand new converts following the apostle Peter's address.

A woman being baptized in the River Jordan.

Baptistery and Font

Many ancient churches, and some very modern ones, have a 'baptistery' – a pool that is deep enough for an adult candidate for baptism to be totally immersed in its water at the moment of baptism. Such a pool is obviously necessary for those churches that practise adult baptism by 'total immersion'.

Other churches have a 'font' – usually a large stone basin with steps up to it – where baptisms take place, the candidate (whether baby or adult) having water poured over them 'in the name of the Father, and of the Son, and of the Holy Spirit'.

The carving on the font of the parish church at Eardisley in England tells the story of Jesus rescuing a sinner and bringing him to God.

Believing and Belonging

Some people begin their journey of faith by believing the Christian message, and then move on into the experience of belonging to the community of believers, the church. Probably more often people begin their journey through some involvement with the church, where they explore the truth claims of Christianity. In that way they eventually bring together faith and membership. In baptism this double commitment is acknowledged, because the candidate professes an inward belief in the gospel, and openly confesses it to the church.

The apostle Paul put this double aspect of commitment very starkly in his letter to the church at Rome: 'If you confess with your lips that Jesus is Lord and believe in your heart that God raised him from the dead, you will be saved' (Romans 10:9).

NAMING

In early times, and today in many cultures, the candidate for baptism receives a new 'baptismal' name. In Italy, for instance, the usual designation on a form for 'first name' is 'baptismal name'. In English-speaking countries this has often been referred to as a 'Christian name'. This practice explains why children who are baptized are often also named in the course of the ceremony.

'CHRISTENING'

Many people refer to baptism as 'christening', but actually this is only a part of the baptism ritual: 'chrism' is the anointing of the candidate with oil, a practice followed in many but by no means all churches today.

Babies and Baptism

Should the infant children of Christian parents be baptized? Most Christian churches have said 'yes', but some – Baptist and evangelical churches, for instance – have claimed that only adults, able to make an informed and mature profession of faith, should be baptized. Those who baptize babies appeal to references in the New Testament to whole households being baptized (which would normally include infants – see Acts 16:33 and 1 Corinthians 1:16). The faith of the parents is exercised on behalf of the child, until such time as he or she is able and willing to profess it themselves. Those who do not, cite such incidents as the baptism of the Ethiopian man (Acts 8:36–38) and Paul's words to the Romans (Romans 10:9) about publicly confessing the faith.

Baptizing a child in an Orthodox church in Athens.

SOME BAPTISMS THAT CHANGED HISTORY

THE EMPEROR CONSTANTINE

The conversion of the Roman emperor Constantine, after his defeat of his rival Maxentius in 312 CE, which he saw as the response of the 'Christian God' to his prayers, changed the whole history of the church. From being widely persecuted, the church and the Christian faith became the favoured religion of the Roman empire. In line with the practice of the time, Constantine was not baptized until later in life (to avoid the possibility of 'post-baptismal sin', which was widely believed to be unforgiveable).

Head of the giant statue of the emperor Constantine in the courtyard of the Palazzo dei Conservatori, Rome, Italy.

CLOVIS

Clovis was king of the Franks – Germanic tribes who had held to their pagan beliefs under Roman rule. In about 500 CE, influenced by his Christian wife and buoyed up by his victory over the Alemanni, which he attributed to divine support, he was baptized, along with three thousand of his troops. In line with the custom of the time, his tribes followed him into Christian baptism and an important alliance was forged between Rome and the Germanic people.

AUGUSTINE

Augustine was the public orator in Milan in the fourth century, a leading intellectual and a member of a cult known as the Manichees. Largely through the ministry of Ambrose, bishop of Milan, he was converted to the Christian faith. After preparation he was baptized at Easter 387 CE, and later became an outstanding bishop and teacher of the Christian faith.

Saint Remigius, bishop of Rheims, baptizing and anointing Clovis I, king of the Franks. From a fourteenth-century French manuscript.

Bread and Wine
'THE LORD'S SUPPER'

On the night before his crucifixion Jesus shared the Jewish Passover supper with his friends. By tradition, unleavened bread (made without yeast) is used on this occasion, and several cups of wine are blessed and then consumed. Jesus departed from the usual form of words, however, and said that the bread was his body given for them, and that the wine was his blood shed for the forgiveness of sins. He then told his followers to 'do this' in the future in remembrance of him.

Consequently down the centuries Christians have always broken and eaten bread and shared wine in remembrance of Jesus. This rite is known by various names – the Lord's Supper, Holy Communion, the Breaking of Bread, the Eucharist and the Mass – but whatever the name, it always involves thanksgiving for the bread and wine and then its consumption by the believers who are present.

Christians attach great significance to this sacrament. Most recognize that in it Jesus is present in a special or even unique way, and that through it they are strengthened and nourished in their spiritual lives. This, they believe, is God's 'food for their journey'.

Preparing the matzah, the special unleavened bread eaten by Jews at Passover. Illustration from the *Rothschild Miscellany*, an Italian manuscript from about 1470.

Manna and Meal

One of the great stories of the Old Testament tells of the way God fed the Israelites on their long journey through the desert on their way from Egypt to the promised land. After a few weeks their food had run out, but their leader, Moses, following God's instructions, told the people to gather and eat a fine white substance that they found on the ground each morning. They called this food 'manna', which is simply the Hebrew for 'What is it?'. It tasted like coriander seed and honey, and this became their staple diet during the desert journey.

After the miracle of the feeding of the 5,000 in the Gospels, when Jesus provided food for 5,000 people using only five loaves and two fish, he drew a parallel between the gift of manna in the wilderness and the gift of himself as the 'bread of life'. He said, 'Your ancestors ate the manna in the wilderness, and they died. This is the bread that comes down from heaven, so that one may eat of it and not die. I am the living bread that came down from heaven. Whoever eats of this bread will live forever; and the bread that I will give for the life of the world is my flesh' (John 6:48–51).

As he then went on to speak of 'eating his flesh' and 'drinking his blood' (which shocked many of his hearers), Christians have associated these words with Holy Communion.

Remembrance

'Remembering' and 'remembrance' have special meanings in the language of the Bible. When present-day Jews celebrate the Passover each year, they give thanks that God brought 'them' out of slavery in Egypt. In other words, they remember a past event by making it part of the present.

In the same way, when Christians 'remember' Jesus, and especially his death on the cross, through the Breaking of Bread, they remember a past event by making it part of the present. He did it once, nearly two thousand years ago, but what he did then is effective in their lives now. The past becomes the present.

The Seder plate is central to the Jewish celebration of Passover or Pesach.

The Earliest Account

The earliest record we have of the institution of the Lord's Supper is the one given by the apostle Paul in his first letter to the Corinthians. This is what he wrote:

For I received from the Lord what I also handed on to you, that the Lord Jesus on the night when he was betrayed took a loaf of bread, and when he had given thanks, he broke it and said, 'This is my body that is for you. Do this in remembrance of me.' In the same way he took the cup also, after supper, saying, 'This cup is the new covenant in my blood. Do this, as often as you drink it, in remembrance of me.' For as often as you eat this bread and drink the cup, you proclaim the Lord's death until he comes.

1 CORINTHIANS 11:23–26

WHAT'S IN A NAME?

In Christian churches the command of Jesus to 'do this in remembrance of me' is observed under different names. In the early church, and in some independent churches today, it is known as the 'Breaking of Bread'. Other churches in the Reformed tradition call it the 'Lord's Supper' or Holy Communion. In Anglican and Lutheran churches it is often called the 'Eucharist' and Roman Catholics almost universally call it the 'Mass'.

Where do these names come from?

Breaking of Bread: Acts 2:42

Lord's Supper: 1 Corinthians 11:20

Holy Communion: 1 Corinthians 10:16 (The word translated 'sharing' – koinonia – also means 'fellowship' or 'communion')

Eucharist: 1 Corinthians 11:24 - 'Eucharist' is the Greek word for giving thanks.

Mass: The word 'mass' is a form of the Latin word for 'dismiss'. At the end of the service the believers are 'dismissed' to represent Christ in the world (see John 20:21).

What Happens at a Communion Service?

Nearly every Christian church has a table in a prominent place (often called an 'altar' or 'altar-table'). At some stage of the service (which normally includes the reading of Scripture, a homily, prayer and worship in song), bread and wine will be placed on the table – the bread may be normal household bread, large wafers of unleavened bread to be broken, or small individual wafers. Usually the wine will be placed in one or more large cups, often known as chalices.

A priest or minister will preside, and at the appropriate time will say the same words as Jesus used at the Last Supper with his friends. He or she will give thanks for the bread and wine, break the bread before the people and invite them to receive the bread and share the cup. When all have received, the table is cleared and the congregation is dismissed with a blessing.

What Christians Believe About the Bread and Wine

Roman Catholics, and Greek and Russian Orthodox Christians, believe that by a miraculous inner change of substance ('transubstantiation') the bread and wine actually become the flesh and blood of Jesus, while remaining outwardly bread and wine.

Christians in the Lutheran, Anglican and Methodist traditions (and many others in the Reformed or Presbyterian churches) generally believe that if the bread and wine are taken and received with faith then the recipient actually (though inwardly) feeds on the body and blood of Jesus.

Other Christians see the rite as solely an act of remembrance, with the bread and wine vivid symbols to awaken faith and encourage the believer to draw closer to Jesus.

Christianity in Art
'SOMETHING BEAUTIFUL FOR GOD'

The second of the Ten Commandments states bluntly that it is 'idolatry' to make the image of anything in heaven, on earth or even 'under the earth' as an object of worship, and all through their history the Jewish people have considered that the commandment ruled out pictorial representations of people or animals. When the Israelites made a golden calf in the desert (while Moses was absent up the mountain receiving the Law), they were to pay a fearful penalty for their action. At the same time, the Tabernacle and later the Temple were lavishly and beautifully decorated, and the Bible gave strict instructions about the materials, colours and methods that were to be used in that decoration. Artists, weavers, sculptors and painters were to be employed, and in the Holy Place, right at the heart of Jewish worship, there would be the carved gold cherubim. These 'representations' of heavenly beings were permitted because they were not there to be worshipped, but to instil in the people a sense of reverence in the presence of God.

In this way, art became an element in worship, though the precise boundary between art as awe and wonder and art as a temptation to idolatry has always troubled the religious mind.

Art in the Early Church

The earliest Christian art was symbolical: a fish represented Christ; a ship stood for the church. However, despite the commandment warning against the making of 'images', Christians began to make representations of biblical events and people, including Jesus and his mother. It's unlikely that these bear any resemblance to their actual appearance, but they were seen as aids to devotion. In the Eastern church this art took the form of iconography, which avoids the charge of idolatry by consciously *not* setting out to portray the actual person, whether saint or angel, but to express something of their character or holiness. Icons were regarded as aids to worship and means of grace, but were not themselves to be objects of worship.

A distinction came to be made between *dulia*, which was the worship or honour that could rightly be accorded to the saints, and *latria*, which was the worship due only to God. Later in the Middle Ages a third category was proposed, *hyperdulia*, which was worship or reverence of the Blessed Virgin Mary.

By such distinctions, it became possible for religious art to be accepted and welcomed, so that by the Middle Ages the bulk of the work of Western artists involved paintings or sculptures of biblical scenes, saints and especially the Virgin Mary.

The highly decorated interior of Shipka Memorial Church, Bulgaria.

Art in Church

The decoration of church buildings became a feature of Christian art from about the fourth century. This was especially true of Byzantine churches (those associated with Constantinople and its patriarch).

The artistic decoration of churches took many different forms – stained glass, wall paintings, engravings, statues and so on – but was seen as a visual aid for the teaching of the faith. People who could not read, and did not understand Latin, learned the biblical stories and the lives of the saints from what they saw in church. The Protestant Reformers generally were suspicious of such art, feeling that it encouraged idolatry, though stained glass has usually been exempt from criticism.

GREAT CHRISTIAN ARTISTS

Giotto (1267–1337): Italian painter. Rejecting the formality characteristic of late Byzantine religious art in Italy, he daringly introduced a note of drama and realism into his work. The frescoes in the Basilica of Francis in Assisi combine energy, colour and action in telling the story of the saint's life. He also painted frescoes in Padua and Florence.

Andrei Rublev (1360–1430): Russian painter of icons. His most famous work is the *Old Testament Trinity*, painted for Trinity Cathedral, near Moscow. It shows the three strangers welcomed by

Icon with the Trinity by Andrei Rublev, Russia, early fourteenth century.

The Adoration of the Magi, by Peter Paul Rubens, 1610.

Madonna and Child with Pope Sixtus II and Saint Barbara, painted around 1512 by Raphael as the altarpiece of the San Sisto monastery, Piacenza, Italy.

Peter Paul Rubens (1577–1640): Flemish painter. A devout Catholic, his *Adoration* (in the chapel of King's College Cambridge) and his tryptych in Antwerp Cathedral reveal a profound understanding of what it meant for Christ to be human, and the meaning of his sacrifice on the cross.

Raphael (1483–1520): Italian Renaissance painter. He was appointed chief architect of St Peter's, Rome. His most famous works include several paintings of the Virgin Mary, including the *Sistine Madonna* and the *Madonna della Sedia*.

Abraham, who turned out to be angelic messengers (Genesis 18:1–15).

Michelangelo (1475–1564): Italian artist whose paintings and sculptures are among the great art treasures of Rome. In 1500 he carved the famous *Pieta* (Mary nursing the body of her dead Son); he completed his sculpture *David* in 1504 and later painted the frescoes on the ceiling of the Sistine Chapel and the *Last Judgment* on the altar wall.

The Pre-Raphaelites (formed 1848): English artists who formed a 'brotherhood' to promote 'fidelity to nature', which they claimed typified Italian art before Raphael. Among them were the painters D.G. Rossetti, Millais and Holman Hunt, and Byrne Jones, who worked largely in stained glass. Among their best-known works are Holman Hunt's *The Scapegoat* and *The Light of the World*.

Solemn Songs
SACRED MUSIC

As far back as anyone can research, human beings have used music and singing in their acts of religious worship. The Temple in Jerusalem resounded to all kinds of music, played on an enormous variety of instruments, accompanying the singing of priests and people and often supplemented by clapping hands. Later, sacred texts were chanted in the synagogue and the Psalms were sung.

The Christian era soon saw the introduction of new texts and eventually an entirely new form of music, though 'plainsong' and chanting, very much in the style of the Jewish Temple, have always been a part of it. Some of the greatest music of Western civilization has been written for sacred use – almost every serious composer until modern times wrote a setting for the Mass or, like Handel, an oratorio or cantata. Even today, in a more secular society, composers still set biblical or other Christian texts to music for choirs and soloists, and their music often has wide appeal, even among people who make no religious profession. It is as though the human ear can recognize a spiritual quality in this music that it cannot find anywhere else.

MUSIC IN THE EARLY CHURCH

We know from the letters of the apostle Paul that Christians joined together in song, possibly spontaneously – 'psalms, hymns and spiritual songs' (Colossians 3:16). What we don't know is whether they continued to sing the chants of the synagogue, though almost certainly congregations of Jewish background would have done so.

As we shall see in the next chapter, hymns were introduced in about the fifth century, but there is no record of anything like the kind of sacred music that emerged with the growing sophistication of the Renaissance period.

FROM THE VERY START...

According to the book of Genesis, one of Noah's descendants, Jubal, was the forerunner of all those through history who would play both stringed instruments ('the lyre') and woodwind ('the pipe') (Genesis 4:12). This certainly suggests that music-making was practised from the days of the patriarchs (the 'first fathers' of Israel), if not earlier.

King David playing the lyre. A mosaic from the floor of the fourth-century AD synagogue at Gaza.

WORSHIP IN THE TEMPLE

Worship in the Temple in Jerusalem in biblical times certainly included music, though perhaps not of the kind we associate with cathedrals! Judging by Psalm 150 it could involve a cacophony of instruments: trumpets, lutes, harps, tambourines, two sorts of cymbals ('clanging' and 'loud'), strings and pipes. There was also singing, of course, which would have involved the chanting of psalms.

Plainsong

Plainsong became the standard accompaniment of formal Christian worship from quite early times – it was well established by the sixth century. It is a way of putting sacred texts to music that conveys dignity, simplicity and discipline. Although the 'performance' of plainsong is devoid of any embellishments or emotional interpretation, its cool innocence conveys to many people a unique kind of spirituality. It is centred mostly on just four notes in the usual scale: D, E, F and G.

Plainsong was the usual form of worship in monastic communities during the Middle Ages.

In the early Middle Ages there were several different forms of plainsong, sometimes to meet the need of different liturgical texts (forms of worship): Ambrosian (from Milan); Gallican (from Gaul); Mozarabic; and Old Roman. Plainsong continued to be the normal accompaniment of the Roman Catholic Mass up to the time of the Second Vatican Council in 1965, but it is still widely used in monasteries and convents.

SOME GREAT COMPOSERS OF SACRED MUSIC

From the late Middle Ages onwards, composers frequently wrote settings for the Mass, or whole works setting out biblical themes. Here are some of the most widely recognized:

Guillaume Dufay (c. 1400–74): Franco-Flemish composer and singer, member of papal choir in Rome. Works include several masses, including a requiem mass, and other church music, some accompanied by instruments.

Claude Goudimel (1510–72): French composer, first of Roman Catholic music, then, after becoming a Protestant, settings for psalms. Killed in a massacre of Protestants.

William Byrd (1543–1623): English composer. Wrote music both for the 'new' Church of England services and for the Roman Catholic mass – he composed three masses as well as many motets (short choral pieces).

Johann Sebastian Bach (1685–1750): German composer. Among his greatest religious works are the *Mass in B Minor* and the *St John Passion*.

George Frideric Handel (1685–1759): German composer who settled in England. His great religious oratorios include *Messiah* and *Judas Maccabaeus*.

Franz Joseph Haydn (1732–1809): Austrian composer. A prolific output – over 100 symphonies – included such religious works as *The Creation*.

Ludwig van Beethoven (1770–1827): German composer. Among his many masterpieces is the *Mass in D*.

Gabriel Fauré (1845–1924): French composer. Among many works including operas and songs he wrote a notable *Requiem* (mass for the departed).

Antonin Dvorak

Antonin Dvorak (1841–1904): Czech composer. Among his many religious works are a *Requiem*, a *Te Deum* and the *Mass in D Major*. He began his career as organist at St Adalbert's Church, Prague.

The choir of Winchester Cathedral, England.

Gabriel Fauré

John Tavener (born 1944): English composer. Having converted to the Russian Orthodox Church in his fifties, Tavener has composed many works in the Orthodox tradition, including *Kontakion*, *Akathist of Thanksgiving*, the *Orthodox Vigil* service and a choral work *Athene*, sung at the funeral of Diana, Princess of Wales.

Hymns and Songs
LET THE PEOPLE SING

As we've seen, there is solemn sacred music, some of it to be traced back to worship in the Temple in Jerusalem, but there has also always been a more spontaneous and 'popular' style of music in worship. The apostle Paul encouraged the Christians at Colosse in Greece to sing 'psalms, hymns and spiritual songs', which suggests quite a wide variety of musical styles. In the churches of the first few centuries this mixture of music continued, though in public worship most of what was sung was either liturgical texts (the words of the service) or psalms. The 'hymns and spiritual songs' were kept for what the New Testament calls 'epi-synagogues' – 'extra' meetings, probably in people's homes.

It was the church in Milan in the fourth century that first introduced 'hymns', more or less as we know them, into regular worship in the West, copying a practice already common in the Eastern church. A few of those early hymns survive in translation in modern hymnbooks, taking their places alongside the bewildering range of music on offer in Christian churches today.

An Early Christian Hymn

To be sung at evening, at the lighting of the lamps:

Hail, gladdening Light, of his pure glory poured
Who is the eternal Father, heavenly, blest,
Holiest of holies, Jesus Christ our Lord.

Now we are come to the sun's hour of rest,
The lights of evening round us shine,
We hymn the Father, Son and Holy Spirit divine.

Worthiest art thou at all times to be sung
With undefiled tongue,
Son of our God, giver of life, alone:
Therefore in all the world thy glories, Lord, they own.
GREEK, THIRD CENTURY

SOME HYMN-WRITERS AND THEIR HYMNS

Thomas Aquinas (1227–74):
Now my tongue the mystery telling*

Martin Rinkart (1586–1649):
Now thank we all our God*

Martin Luther (1483–1546):
Ein' Feste Burg ('A safe stronghold')*

Paul Gerhardt (1607–76):
O sacred head, surrounded*

Isaac Watts (1674–1748):
O God our help in ages past
Come let us join our cheerful songs

Katherina Von Schlegal (b. 1697):
Be still, my soul*

Charles Wesley (1707–1788):
Love divine
Hark the herald angels sing

William Williams (1717–91):
Guide me, O thou great Redeemer*

John Ellerton (1826–93):
The day thou gavest, Lord, is ended

Cecil Frances Alexander (1818–95):
All things bright and beautiful
There is a green hill far away
Once in royal David's city

Fanny J. Crosby (1820–1915):
Blessed assurance, Jesus is mine

Christina Rossetti (1830–94):
In the bleak mid-winter

Ira D. Sankey (1840–1908):
There were ninety and nine that safely lay

Karl Boberg (1859–1940):
How great thou art*

Timothy Dudley-Smith (b. 1926):
Tell out, my soul

Graham Kendrick (b. 1950):
From heaven you came, helpless babe

* TRANSLATION (FROM GERMAN, LATIN, SWEDISH OR WELSH)

Statue of Paul Gerhardt at Mittenwalde, Germany.

Portrait of Christina Rossetti by W. A. Mansell.

● SEE ALSO
SOLEMN SONGS P96-97
WORSHIP P34-35

MUSIC FROM TAIZÉ

Taizé is an ecumenical monastic community in western France founded in 1940 by Brother Roger. It has attracted vast numbers of pilgrims, including many young people from all over the world. The worship at Taizé has pioneered a form of music that has been used extensively throughout the world-wide church. It sets simple texts, often in Latin, to repetitive tunes that can be sung or chanted in unison or harmony. Many are based on biblical sayings or themes, and when used locally they are easily translated into other languages. Taizé chants are used in worship right across the Christian denominations.

Ecumenical worship at Taizé, France.

WORSHIP SONGS

A feature of worship in the post-charismatic era has been the widespread introduction of 'worship songs', often accompanied by drums, guitars and other instruments rather than the traditional organ. Although first used in churches influenced by the charismatic or Pentecostal movement, they are now regularly sung in churches of all traditions. Many worship songs originated in the USA and subsequently in Britain and Europe, and were popularized on the radio or through records.

The range of worship songs is enhanced by the inclusion of 'spirituals', the songs of the slaves in the cotton plantations in America ('Swing low, sweet chariot'), and more recently by worship songs of Caribbean and African origin.

AMBROSE OF MILAN

In the fourth century the great preacher Ambrose ('the silver-tongued') was bishop of the church in Milan. He introduced hymns to the congregation there, the first time they had been used in public worship in the Western church. He himself wrote a number of hymns, at least one of which is still sung ('O Strength and Stay'). Augustine, then the public orator in Milan, was passing the church one day and heard the singing, which attracted him to enter and then hear Ambrose preach. This was the beginning of his journey to Christian conversion.

Faith Under Fire

THE RISE OF SECULARISM

There have always been people who don't believe in God, some 'agnostics' (literally 'don't knows') and some 'atheists' (non-believers). Until modern times, however, they have usually been a small and more or less silent minority. Since the twentieth century, and especially since the Theory of Evolution was widely accepted, there has been much more religious scepticism and a growing body of opinion in Europe particularly that religion is not simply wrong (as an explanation of the way the world is), but misleading and damaging.

Marxists and secular humanists have long believed that advances in scientific understanding would give birth to a society in which religion would simply fade away. It hasn't happened, and the world of the twenty-first century is probably more aggressively 'religious' than any since the Middle Ages. Yet while humanists and atheists are still a minority in almost every culture, apart from the officially anti-religious regimes in countries such as China and North Korea, they have many articulate proponents. They often set what they would call 'scientific fact' over against religious belief, and have made Christians, especially, rethink the way in which they present their faith in a society that is more ready to challenge not just its relevance but also its truth.

SECULARISM

Secularism is an approach that seeks to order life solely on principles taken from this world, without reference to God or religion. ('Secular' is based on the Latin word for 'world'.) In recent times it has been used in a broader sense to describe an outlook or lifestyle that denies or ignores religious ideas.

Some of the finches studied by Charles Darwin on his visit to the Galapagos Islands in 1835. Their distinctive beaks led Darwin to postulate that they may have been adapted as a result of different diets.

ORNITHOLOGY. 457

1. Geospiza magnirostris.
3. Geospiza parvula.

2. Geospiza fortis.
4. Certhidea olivacea.

Some controversial advances in science have raised ethical issues and have resulted in conflict with religious belief. Dolly, the world's first cloned sheep, is seen on the right.

The God of the Gaps

Until fairly recent times, Christians tended to defend their position over against scientific discovery by emphasizing those things that science could not explain – a technique often described as the 'God of the Gaps' defence. What brought the first matter into existence? Why (in the question posed by Stephen Hawking) does the universe bother to exist? The weakness of the argument is that the 'gaps' steadily shrink as scientific discovery bit by bit offers explanations for the hitherto inexplicable: laboratory creation of living organisms, cloning and genetic research, for instance. Scientists who are themselves believers have warned for a long while that better arguments are needed than a retreat into narrower and narrower 'gaps'.

Thinking About Science, Truth and Faith
● ● ● ● ● ● ● ● ● ● ● ● ● ● ●

'It is extraordinary that anything should exist at all. Surely the most natural state of affairs is simply nothing: no universe, no God, nothing. But there is something... If we can explain the many bits of the universe by one simple being which keeps them in existence, we should do so – even if inevitably we cannot explain the existence of that simple being.'

RICHARD SWINBURNE, PROFESSOR OF PHILOSOPHY, UNIVERSITY OF OXFORD

'The power of science is precisely because it's adaptable; it improves all the time. Scientific enquiry mirrors, albeit in some imperfect but improving way, a really existing order in nature. I think evidence for something like meaning or purpose or design in the universe comes from the demystification of nature through scientific enquiry.'

PAUL DAVIES, PHYSICIST, UNIVERSITY OF ADELAIDE, AUSTRALIA

'Increasing knowledge of science without a corresponding growth of religious wisdom only increases our fear of death.'

SARVEPALLI RADHAKRISHNAN, PROFESSOR OF RELIGION, UNIVERSITY OF OXFORD

'Science without religion is lame, religion without science is blind.'

ALBERT EINSTEIN, THEORETICAL PHYSICIST

'Science is built of facts the way a house is built of bricks; but an accumulation of facts is no more science than a pile of bricks is a house.'

HENRI POINCARE, MATHEMATICIAN AND PHYSICIST, UNIVERSITY OF PARIS

Galileo argued for a sun-centred universe at a time when many leading Catholics still supported the view of an earth-centred one. The arguments were further inflamed by different interpretations of biblical references.

Science Versus Faith?
● ●

To pose 'science' (which simply means 'knowledge') over against 'faith' (which means trust in a divine power) is a simplistic approach to the question of truth. After all, many thousands of the world's most brilliant scientists are in fact Christians, and they are found in every scientific discipline – physics, biology, cosmology and chemistry. Clearly they do not see it as a crude choice between believing seven impossible things before breakfast and maintaining scientific detachment. Most of them would say that science is answering the 'how' questions, and faith the equally important 'why' questions. Once it is established *how* something came to be so, the question remains (and will always remain) as to *why* it should be so. Faith looks for answers to questions that by their very nature lie outside the domain of science. They have to do with the purpose of our existence, the possibility of 'meaning' to our lives and the undeniable presence of something we can call the 'spiritual' in our understanding of reality.

CHRISTIANITY: GOOD OR BAD?

Richard Dawkins, an Oxford professor, has written a best-selling book arguing that religion is a negative influence in the world, and that we would be better off without it. How does Christianity rate on this test?

Christianity Bad

■ Wars of religion (e.g. Crusades).

■ Exploitation or subjugation of women.

■ Failure to condemn such things as slavery, racial and caste prejudice.

■ Abuse of power by religious leaders.

■ Denial of freedom of thought, experiment or belief (e.g. Galileo, the Inquisition).

Christianity Good

■ Teaching of Jesus calls for peace, justice and mercy – 'love your enemies'.

■ Jesus treated men and women equally – eventually the churches have responded to his example.

■ Christians led the fight for the abolition of slavery in the USA, the British empire and elsewhere. Eventually, the churches also accepted what the apostle Paul said about different races being 'all one in Christ'.

■ Christians founded hospitals, schools, orphanages and hospices where none existed previously.

■ Jesus clearly taught that leadership is service, not dominance. Those who ignore this are rejecting his teaching.

■ The Renaissance and the whole explosion of scientific experiment and philosophical debate occurred in the Christian West.

Christians and War

SWORDS INTO PLOUGHSHARES?

Issues of war and peace have always been a problem for Christians and for the Christian church. This is partly because, as we shall see, the teaching of Jesus is so clearly against violence of any kind, even in a good cause, and partly because the church has to live in the real world, where wars happen – and when they do, they demand that people decide whether to support one side or the other, or declare themselves 'neutral'. In case the latter may sound the wise and Christian option, it's worth pointing out that sometimes to be 'neutral' is effectively to give support to one side rather than the other. Those who claimed to be 'neutral' in the Second World War, for instance, might be accused of standing by while Hitler and his armies put the world under a totalitarian yoke.

On the whole, throughout Christian history the church's record on issues of war and peace has not been a very good one. Its priests have blessed armies going into battle, and even nuclear submarines. It has supported religious wars and sometimes encouraged its members to take up arms in the name of Christ, as in the Crusades of the Middle Ages. At the same time, there has been a strong element of pacifism in Christianity: there have always been Christians who have stood out against the use of force, especially when it is used to defend or extend the 'kingdom of God'.

What Jesus Taught About War and Peace

'Put your sword back into its place; for all who take the sword will perish by the sword.'
MATTHEW 26:52

'You have heard that it was said, "An eye for an eye and a tooth for a tooth." But I say to you, Do not resist an evildoer. But if anyone strikes you on the right cheek, turn the other also.'
MATTHEW 5:38, 39

'You have heard that it was said, "You shall love your neighbour and hate your enemy." But I say to you, Love your enemies and pray for those who persecute you, so that you may be children of your Father in heaven.'
MATTHEW 5:43, 44

As he came near Jerusalem and saw the city, he wept over it, saying, 'If you, even you, had only recognized on this day the things that make for peace!'
LUKE 19:42

Jerusalem, the city Jesus wept over, viewed from the Mount of Olives.

What People Have Said About War

'For a Christian who believes in Jesus and his gospel, war is an iniquity and a contradiction.'
POPE JOHN XXIII

'The Church knows nothing of the sacredness of war. The Church which prays "Our Father" asks God only for peace.'
DIETRICH BONHOEFFER

'A good portion of the evils that afflict mankind is due to the erroneous belief that life can be made secure by violence.'
LEO TOLSTOY

'As peace is of all goodness, so war is an emblem, a hieroglyphic, of all misery.'
JOHN DONNE

'The modern choice is between non-violence or non-existence.'
MARTIN LUTHER KING

'War can only be a desperate remedy in a desperate situation, used to spare humanity a still greater evil.'
RENÉ COSTE

● SEE ALSO
'HOLY' WARS P64-65

Christians and War

Despite the teaching of Jesus, the attitude of Christians and of the church to war has been ambivalent. Both Paul and Peter urge believers to respect the civil authorities and honour the emperor (see Romans 13:1–4 and 1 Peter 2:17), even though the church was always on a knife-edge in its relationship with Rome and persecution of Christians was widespread from apostolic times onwards. Paul was once rescued from a mob by military intervention (Acts 23:26, 27) and there were Christians who were soldiers in the Roman army from the second century onwards. From the time of the conversion of Constantine in 312 CE Christians were less troubled by the idea of participation in war. Many, though not all, Christians argued that the use of force was sometimes morally justified and even praiseworthy.

In the Middle Ages there were several attempts to draw up guidelines for the church over issues of war and the use of force. In modern times Christian pacifism, the doctrine that the use of force is wrong in all circumstances and plainly contrary to the gospel, has been held by groups of people in all the churches, and by some church leaders. Nevertheless, mainstream Christian thought has reluctantly accepted that in an imperfect world the use of force, and even the waging of war, may sometimes be the 'least bad' option.

An American soldier prays inside an armoured vehicle during a patrol near the Iraqi holy city of Najaf.

The 'Just War'

Thomas Aquinas drew up some principles for what he called a 'Just War' – a war in which it would be proper for Christians to be involved. His three principles were supplemented later by a fourth, devised by de Vitoria, known as the 'Father of International Law'. They are as follows:

1. A Just War must be lawfully authorized.

2. Its cause must be just.

3. The belligerents must have a 'rightful intention' (good motives).

4. It must be waged by 'proper means'.

Many Christians in recent times have felt that such a war is no longer possible in that modern weapons of mass destruction can never be 'proper'. In most wars in the last 50 years more civilians have been killed than military personnel. Another of de Vitoria's principles is relevant today: no war is permissible that brings serious evil to the world at large.

Thomas Aquinas, regarded as the foremost theologian of the Catholic Church. He is portrayed holding an open book, with a dove, representing the Holy Spirit, at his shoulder.

THE 'QUAKERS'

The 'Quakers' is the popular name for the religious movement known as the 'Society of Friends' or, in the USA, very often the 'Friends' Church'. It was born of the religious turmoil in England in the mid-seventeenth century. Its leader, George Fox, rejected the whole idea of ordained ministers and consecrated buildings, emphasizing instead the 'inner light' of Christ within each person. Traditionally Quaker worship has involved a great deal of silence, with spontaneous readings from the Bible or other works, and prayer. They refused to pay tithes, swear oaths or take up arms. This led to persecution by the authorities, and a group of Quakers led by William Penn founded Pennsylvania in America in 1682 as a 'Holy Experiment' in Quaker principles.

In the wars of the last two centuries members of the Society of Friends have refused to take up arms, but have served, often bravely, in ambulance units, and have actively sought to promote peace, justice and international relief.

Christianity and Sex

THE FORBIDDEN FRUIT?

You could say that sex has always been a problem for the human race, a great source of joy and a great cause of anguish. People have fought and died over it, yet some of our greatest literature and art celebrates the beauty of human sexual love. If sex has been a problem for the human race, it's also true that it's been a great problem for the Christian church. The Scriptures and the teaching of Jesus lay down very high standards of sexual behaviour; standards that have consistently eluded some of the greatest figures of the faith – men like David and Solomon, for instance.

The basic biblical principle about sex is laid down in the opening chapters of the first book of the Bible. 'Therefore a man leaves his father and mother, and clings to his wife, and they become one flesh' (Genesis 2:24). This principle of 'one flesh' – a physical union symbolizing a permanent relationship – was endorsed by Jesus, quoting those very words, and has become the touchstone of Christian teaching on the subject from the first.

The trouble has always been that it settles one set of problems, but seems to open up a lot more!

The Old Testament and Sex

You shall not commit adultery.
EXODUS 20:14

You shall not lie with a male as with a woman; it is an abomination.
LEVITICUS 18:22

If a man commits adultery with the wife of his neighbour, both the adulterer and the adulteress shall be put to death.
LEVITICUS 20:10

My beloved is mine and I am his; he pastures his flock among the lilies. Until the day breaks and the shadows flee, turn, my beloved, be like a gazelle or a young stag on the cleft mountains.
SONG OF SOLOMON 2:16, 17

Contradictions or Tensions?

The Old Testament presents what seems to be a contradiction between powerful denunciation of adultery and other departures from the 'one flesh' principle on the one hand, and an acceptance of polygamy (multiple wives, as Jacob, David and Solomon had) and a joyful celebration of sexual love (as found in the *Song of Solomon*) on the other. The early part of the history of Israel is strongly patriarchal – men held all of the power, and having many wives was a sign of wealth and prosperity. Monogamy (having one wife) became the norm about a thousand years before Christ.

In fact the 'contradiction' is a moral tension between the ideal and the achievable. The Bible simply urges us to keep on trying for the best in every area of human relationships.

Five Christian Principles About Sex

1. God's ideal pattern is that sex should always take place between a man and a woman within a loving, stable and permanent relationship – what we call 'marriage'.

2. That relationship is sacred, and those who deliberately or wilfully destroy it are guilty of 'adultery'.

3. The two sexes have equal rights and equal responsibilities in their relationships.

4. Sexual activity that treats the body as a piece of equipment or a plaything is blasphemous. God made the body, and it is 'the temple of the Holy Spirit' (1 Corinthians 6:19). We must treat our own and other people's bodies with reverence.

5. 'Love is the fulfilling of the law,' said the apostle Paul (Romans 13:10). Consequently the defining criterion in sexual behaviour is love.

What Jesus Said About Sex

Lust
Jesus condemned adultery, but went further. Even to 'look at a woman with lust' is a kind of interior adultery (Matthew 5:27).

Divorce
Jesus said that the Law of Moses permitted divorce because of human failure and obstinacy ('hardness of heart'), but that God's original purpose was that marriage should be lifelong. The couple are 'no longer two, but one flesh'. He added, 'What God has joined together, let no one separate' (Mark 10:2–9).

Adultery
While, as we have seen, Jesus condemned adultery, when he was faced with a woman who had been caught in the very act, and invited by those who had brought her to him to authorize her stoning to death (as the Law of Moses required), he did not do so. First he asked those present who were without sin to 'cast the first stone'. Then, when they had all gone away without doing so, he told the women that he did not 'condemn' her, but that she should 'from now on' not sin again (John 8:3–11).

Jesus' opponents used the discovery of a woman caught in the act of adultery as an opportunity to trap him. But he did not condemn the woman, and instead used the situation to remind his questioners that nobody is free from guilt. *Christ and the Woman Taken in Adultery (Who is Without Sin?)* by Vasily Polienov.

What People Have Said About Sex and Religion

'*Sexuality throws no light on love, but only through love can we understand sexuality.*'
EUGEN ROSENSTOCK-HUESSY

'*Whenever Christ was confronted by people in sexual disarray, he took good care to safeguard sexuality by reminding them that they had to avoid sin; that is to say, to use their sexuality in a fully human way.*'
JACK DOMINIAN

'*The degree and kind of a man's sexuality reach up into the ultimate pinnacle of his spirit.*'
FRIEDRICH NIETZSCHE

'*The essence of chastity is not the suppression of lust, but the total orientation of one's life to a goal.*'
DIETRICH BONHOEFFER

'*Sex has become one of the most discussed subjects of modern times. The Victorians pretended it did not exist; the moderns pretend that nothing else exists.*'
FULTON SHEEN

Christianity and Homosexuality

This has become a major issue for the Christian churches, particularly since homosexual relationships have been legalized in most Western countries. Both the Old Testament (Leviticus) and the apostle Paul (in his letters to Corinth and Rome) reject physical homosexual relationships, Paul describing them as 'unnatural' (Romans 1:26, 27). It is interesting that there is no record of Jesus saying anything at all on the subject, even though homosexuality was a major feature of life in the Graeco-Roman world.

The Christian churches have almost unanimously rejected homosexual practice as contrary to biblical teaching, but in recent decades it has been normal to make a distinction between homosexual *orientation*, which for most people is not a matter of choice, and homosexual *practice*. The Roman Catholic position is that gay people should practise sexual abstinence, but the church will view their situation with understanding. The other churches, while maintaining the traditional Christian view that sex is to be enjoyed within a man – woman and lifelong relationship, have tried to find ways of welcoming and affirming the faith of gay people and helping them to 'fulfil the law of love' in ways appropriate to their situation.

Christianity and Alcohol
GOD'S GIFT – OR THE DEVIL'S BREW?

Like sex, alcohol has been a constant source of trouble and anxiety in both Judaism and Christianity. This is because, like sex, it is seen both as a gift of God – he gives wine 'to make glad man's heart' (Psalm 104:15) – and as a moral problem when its use is not controlled. The Bible offers no specific laws or commandments to do with consuming alcohol, but there are plenty of warnings of its dangers when indulged in excessively – and plenty of examples, from Noah onwards, of those who did not heed the warnings.

For Christians there is also the example of Jesus, who evidently drank wine and enjoyed it (Luke 7:34). He even miraculously provided an enormous quantity of wine, about 150 gallons (682 litres) of it, for a friend's wedding feast when supplies had run out. However we interpret this 'sign' in John's Gospel, it does not suggest that Jesus would have supported the temperance movement! However, neither he nor his disciples were ever accused of over-indulgence. His example sets the tone for the general teaching of the New Testament on the subject, and also for subsequent church teaching on alcohol. By all means use it, but do not allow it to use you!

What the Old Testament Says About Alcohol

Wine is a mocker, strong drink a brawler, and whoever is led astray by it is not wise.
PROVERBS 20:1

Give strong drink to one who is perishing, and wine to those in bitter distress; let them drink and forget their poverty, and remember their misery no more.
PROVERBS 31:6

Do not be among winebibbers, or among gluttonous eaters of meat; for the drunkard and the glutton will come to poverty, and drowsiness will clothe them with rags.
PROVERBS 23:20, 21

What the New Testament Says About Alcohol

Do not get drunk with wine, for that is debauchery.
EPHESIANS 5:18

Now a bishop must be above reproach, married only once, temperate, sensible, respectable, hospitable, an apt teacher, not a drunkard, not violent but gentle, not quarrelsome, and not a lover of money.
1 TIMOTHY 3:3

No longer drink only water, but take a little wine for the sake of your stomach and your frequent ailments.
1 TIMOTHY 5:23

You have already spent enough time in doing what the Gentiles like to do, living in licentiousness, passions, drunkenness, revels, carousing, and lawless idolatry. They are surprised that you no longer join them in the same excesses of dissipation, and so they blaspheme.
1 PETER 4:3

● SEE ALSO
SELF-DENIAL P40-41

How Christianity Has Dealt with Alcohol

In the first few centuries: The early Christians were noted for their disciplined lifestyle. They were free to drink wine, but practised moderation in an era when drunkenness was rife.

In the Middle Ages: Excessive consumption of alcohol was variously seen as a sin, a vice and in some countries a crime. Drunkenness among priests and monks was regarded as a scandal. In contrast, many devout Christians, including monks, nuns and priests, took vows of total abstinence from alcohol.

From the late eighteenth century: Drunkenness was a major social problem in many European countries in the eighteenth century, with ale-houses in England advertising 'Drunk for a penny – dead drunk for two pence'. The Methodist Revival was seen as a major factor in countering excessive drinking – most Methodists became total abstainers. At the same time, alcoholism began to be seen as a medical condition. In 1874 Dr Benjamin Rush, one of the signatories of the American Declaration of Independence, wrote a paper called 'An Inquiry into the Effects of Ardent Spirits on the Human Body and Mind'.

In Catholic countries: Alcohol consumption continued to be a problem for some lay-people and clergy, but there were also powerful groups, like the 'Pioneers' in Ireland, who pledged abstinence to atone for the excesses of others. The church generally has taught moderation rather than abstinence.

In Protestant cultures, especially the United States, there has been a strong element of abstinence in Christian teaching, many Christians taking 'the pledge' (to abstain from alcohol in every form). This led many Protestant churches to abandon the use of wine at Holy Communion, and substitute non-alcoholic (unfermented) grape juice. In Victorian Britain alcohol had a destructive effect in the urban slums, the week's wages being spent on drink and families suffering poverty and hunger as a result.

In the USA the manufacture and sale of alcohol was banned by federal law between 1920 and 1933. The experiment failed because of 'boot-legging' – the illegal sale of liquor, often organized by criminal gangs. Here barrels of beer are being emptied into the sewer.

WILLIAM BOOTH

William Booth, born in 1829, was the founder of the Salvation Army. He had moved to London in 1849 for work reasons and in 1865, shocked at the living conditions of the poor in London's East End, founded the 'Christian Mission', which ran soup kitchens for the hungry. In 1878 this became the 'Salvation Army', organized along military lines but without weapons. He launched a 'war' against such evils as alcohol abuse, poverty, prostitution, gambling and bad housing. His book *Darkest England and the Way Out* (1890) offered a programme of social reforms aimed at countering them. The Salvation Army soon spread to the United States, and then across Europe and the Commonwealth. Booth died in 1912.

What People Have Said About Drinking

'Drunkenness is no substitute for happiness. It amounts to buying the dream of a thing when you haven't money enough to buy the dreamed-of thing materially.'
ANDRE GIDE

'Temperance is to the body what religion is to the soul – the foundation of health, strength and peace.'
TYRON EDWARDS

'If we give more to our flesh than we ought, we nourish our enemy; if we give not to her necessity what we ought, we destroy a citizen.'
POPE GREGORY I

'Temperance is corporal piety; it is the preservation of divine order in the body.'
THEODORE PARKER

'Drink not the third glass, which thou canst not tame when once it is within thee.'
GEORGE HERBERT

Christianity, Crime and Punishment
MERCY TRIUMPHS OVER JUDGMENT?

A religion whose central principles are forgiveness and redemption is always going to have to struggle with issues of crime and punishment. If the heart of Christianity is to call people to repent, to be forgiven and to start a new life in Christ, what place does a criminal code or a penal system have in that? When Jesus forgave the soldiers who crucified him, or the thief hanging next to him on a cross, did that mean that they were no longer to be held responsible for what they had done? Is punishment a Christian response to evil? And if not, what would Christians put in its place?

Questions like these have exercised Christian thinkers and leaders down the centuries. Christianity is the child of a religion, Judaism, which treasures the law, seeing it as a 'way' to the good life. Can there be another path, which does not involve law-breaking and punishment? Or is it a caricature of Christianity to think of it as a religion without rules, a kind of soft free-for-all in which the sinner is always forgiven and the guilty are always redeemed? After all, the Jesus who is the Saviour of the world and the forgiver of sinners is also, according to the New Testament, the one who will be our Judge.

ARBITRARY JUDGMENT?

The principle was accepted by New Testament writers and even by Jesus – see Matthew 5:25, 26. Its merit is that it is fair: the penalty is laid down, the offence has been committed and the offender pays the price of his or her sin. Its weakness can lie in an arbitrary application of the penalties, without regard to mitigating circumstances, though in that respect Jesus took a different approach (see John 8:11).

The 'retributive' attitude to punishment went virtually unchallenged through history until the last two hundred years, and was enshrined in much church teaching.

'Retributive justice' at work. A Puritan offender in the stocks at Massachusetts Bay Colony in the seventeenth century.

PUNISHMENT AS A MEANS TO AN END

From the eighteenth century onwards some Christians have been unhappy about retribution as the sole aim of punishment. They have felt that the Christian gospel inevitably includes also an element of redemption – amendment of life, an opportunity to put past sin and failure behind us and start again. It's not been easy to accommodate the two views of punishment, and inevitably some people have felt that it must be entirely the one or entirely the other. However, those (like Jeremy Bentham) who wished to change the penal system in the direction of deterrence, reformation and rehabilitation also accepted that crime needed to be punished, and many of those who believed in the principle of 'just deserts' also wished to see criminals reformed. In the last 50 years it has been commonplace to see the two views working in a complementary way.

Two prisoners studying in the library of a prison in the Urals, Russia.

What People Have Said About Crime and Punishment

Those who spare the rod hate their children, but those who love them are diligent to discipline them.
PROVERBS 13:24

'*He only may chastise who loves.*'
RABINDRANATH TAGORE

'*Whipping and abuse are like laudanum; you have to double the dose as the sensibilities decline.*'
HARRIET BEECHER STOWE

'*Speaking generally, punishment hardens and numbs, it produces concentration, it sharpens the consciousness of alienation, it strengthens the power of resistance.*'
FRIEDRICH NIETZSCHE

'*The real significance of crime is in its being a breach of faith with the community of mankind.*'
JOSEPH CONRAD

'*Nothing in this lost world bears the impress of the Son of God so surely as forgiveness.*'
ALICE CAREY

An illustration from 1900 appearing in the French newspaper *Le Petit Parisien* of a garotting in Spain.

GETTING WHAT WE DESERVE

For most of human history, and certainly in the history of all our great religious faiths, the central element of punishment of an offender has been retribution; that's to say, regarding the person as deserving punishment because of the offence they have committed. To put it crudely, offenders get what they deserve. So all through the Law of Moses in the Old Testament the offence is described and then the penalty is laid down. Many of these were very severe: stoning to death, bodily mutilation or substantial compensation to be paid to the person wronged.

FYODOR DOSTOEVSKY

Fyodor Dostoevsky was a Russian novelist (1821–81) whose works had a profound influence among Russian Orthodox theologians and on the thinking of the Lutheran Karl Barth. Dostoevsky's own deep religious experience had convinced him that salvation was the free gift of God to the weak and miserable – a salvation to which a person could bring nothing but their own need of it. His principle of boundless compassion coloured his approach to crime, as well as everyday acts of sin or wickedness. For him, punishment was pointless; the answer was always generous love and acceptance.

CHUCK COLSON

Charles ('Chuck') Colson was an aide to the former US president Robert Nixon, and was involved in the Watergate conspiracy of 1972, for which he served a prison sentence. While in prison he rediscovered his Christian faith and determined to dedicate the rest of his life to a programme of rehabilitation, support and reform for those who had committed crimes and had been imprisoned. In his approach he balanced the 'retributive' view (the criminal gets what he deserves) with the reformist one, that the complementary objective of punishment must be the reform of the offenders and giving them the opportunity to start a new life. For him, this was best achieved by the Christian values of repentance, faith, mercy and forgiveness. His prison ministry has been widely acclaimed in the USA and is now found in many Western countries.

Chuck Colson, imprisoned for his part in Watergate, addresses prisoners at the New Hampshire State Prison with other Christians from Operation Starting Line.

Christians and Poverty
'BLESSED ARE THE POOR'

There's a lot about 'the poor' in the Bible, mainly because most people in biblical times fell into that category – alongside a few people who were indescribably rich. People scratched a living from the soil and from keeping a few animals, with parcels of land passed on from father to son. This meant that eventually the pieces available to each descendant became smaller and smaller, unless they made enough money to buy extra land. When Jesus told his hearers not to worry about what they should eat, he was addressing a major daily anxiety. When he fed the crowds with bread and fish, hordes followed him, because a free and endless supply of food would transform their lives.

This is the setting for the Bible's teaching on poverty, which has provided the fundamental Christian approach to the subject. God fed his people in the desert with manna, and Jesus fed the crowds with fish and bread; but as far as the Hebrew Scriptures were concerned, the great 'banquet' lay in the future, in the coming age of God's blessing. Until then, people are called upon to share what they have, to 'remember the poor' and to treat their daily bread with reverence and gratitude.

Poverty in America. A Salvation Army officer distributes cups of buttermilk to jobless men in New York, around 1900.

What Jesus Said About the Poor

'Blessed are you who are poor, for yours is the kingdom of God.'
LUKE 6:20

Jesus answered them, 'Go and tell John what you hear and see: the blind receive their sight, the lame walk, the lepers are cleansed, the deaf hear, the dead are raised, and the poor have good news brought to them.'
MATTHEW 11:4, 5

'You always have the poor with you, and you can show kindness to them whenever you wish; but you will not always have me.'
MARK 14:7

Jesus, looking at (the rich young man), loved him and said, 'You lack one thing; go, sell what you own, and give the money to the poor, and you will have treasure in heaven; then come, follow me.' When he heard this, he was shocked and went away grieving, for he had many possessions.
MARK 10:19–21

'When you give a luncheon or a dinner, do not invite your friends or your brothers or your relatives or rich neighbours, in case they may invite you in return, and you would be repaid. But when you give a banquet, invite the poor, the crippled, the lame, and the blind. And you will be blessed, because they cannot repay you, for you will be repaid at the resurrection of the righteous.'
LUKE 14:12, 13

Christian Teaching on Poverty

1. Poverty can be a 'blessing', in that those who are poor have a sense of dependence that those who are wealthy are denied.

2. Poverty can be a curse, because it degrades humanity, deprives people of the basic necessities of life, and makes sheer survival its only goal.

3. Those who have much should share it with those who have little, as a matter of Christian obedience (see Acts 2:44, 45 and 2 Corinthians 8:13–15).

4. Christian employers should pay fair wages (James 5:4, 5).

5. The care of the elderly and dependent widows is a primary duty for Christians (1 Timothy 5:8).

6. The Christian church has a special duty to care for the poor, marginalized, handicapped and weak, following the example of Christ. This may involve political and social action of a direct kind.

What People Have Said About Poverty

Those who oppress the poor insult their Maker, but those who are kind to the needy honour him.
PROVERBS 14:31

'No man should praise poverty but he who is poor.'
BERNARD OF CLAIRVAUX

'Forgive us for pretending to care for the poor, when we do not like poor people and do not want them in our homes.'
LITANY OF THE UNITED PRESBYTERIAN CHURCH

For if a person with gold rings and in fine clothes comes into your assembly, and if a poor person in dirty clothes also comes in, and if you take notice of the one wearing the fine clothes and say, 'Have a seat here, please,' while to the one who is poor you say, 'Stand there,' or, 'Sit at my feet,' have you not made distinctions among yourselves, and become judges with evil thoughts?
JAMES 2:2–4

If a brother or sister is naked and lacks daily food, and one of you says to them, 'Go in peace; keep warm and eat your fill,' and yet you do not supply their bodily needs, what is the good of that?
JAMES 2:15, 16

'If a free society cannot help the many who are poor, it cannot save the few who are rich.'
JOHN F. KENNEDY

St Bernard of Clairvaux (c.1090–1153), French Cistercian monk and abbot of Clairvaux, carrying a model of the monastery chapel.

MOTHER TERESA OF CALCUTTA

Mother Teresa (Agnes Gonxha Bojaxhiu) was born in Macedonia in 1910 of Albanian parents. She joined the Sisters of Loretto in 1928 and was sent to Calcutta, to teach at a school for the wealthy. However, in 1948 she was allowed to leave her Order. Dressed in a sari, she went to live in the city's slums, teaching the children of the very poor and caring for the destitute. Joined by others, she founded the Missionary Sisters of Charity and worked among the poorest people – mostly with the dying – until her own death in 1997. She was given a state funeral.

CLARE OF ASSISI

In the early thirteenth century the 18-year-old Clare came under the influence of Francis in the town of Assisi. Inspired by his teaching she renounced possessions and took on the life of a Benedictine nun. With the help of Francis she was eventually able to set up a separate house at San Damiano, near Assisi, following Franciscan principles of poverty and service. Her nuns followed a life of extreme austerity, serving the poor of the district, also following Francis in his concern for the whole created order. She survived Francis, though in poor health, and after her death the Order – the 'Minoresses', or more popularly 'Poor Clares' – spread to many lands in Europe. By stipulating that the only support for the Order should be by alms (which should not include money), she ensured that unlike some other medieval communities they never became corporately wealthy.

St Clare of Assisi, painted by Memmo di Filipuccio in the fourteenth century.

Christians and Slavery
'TO SET THE CAPTIVE FREE'

Slavery was a universal element in the life of the people of the Bible, as it was throughout the then known world. Men and women were taken into slavery through conquest, people fell into slavery through poverty, and some were simply born into slavery. The Law of Moses accepted slavery as a part of the social order and confined itself to moderating its bad influences and ensuring some kind of rough justice for slaves. In the famous story in Genesis, Joseph (the 'Dreamer') was sold into slavery in Egypt by his own brothers. Right through to relatively modern times, it was widely argued that society could not survive economically without slavery, so while the apostle Paul, for example, urged Christian slave owners to treat their believing slaves as 'brothers and sisters in Christ', he held back from insisting that they should be set free. Slaves should be treated well, but unless they could purchase their release they were slaves for life.

Jesus said nothing about slavery as a feature of social order, but he did describe his disciples' ministry in terms of slavery ('Whoever wants to be first must be slave of all'), and at the Last Supper he took upon himself the role of a slave in washing his disciples' feet.

Slavery and the Old Testament

In the Old Testament, the principle of slavery is not questioned, but the Law provides rules about the treatment of slaves, and means by which they can be released from slavery. However, there is never any doubt that the slave is the possession of his or her 'owner'.

When a slave-owner strikes a male or female slave with a rod and the slave dies immediately, the owner shall be punished. But if the slave survives a day or two, there is no punishment; for the slave is the owner's property.
EXODUS 21:20

When a slave-owner strikes the eye of a male or female slave, destroying it, the owner shall let the slave go, a free person, to compensate for the eye.
EXODUS 21:26

If a member of your community, whether a Hebrew man or a Hebrew woman, is sold to you and works for you six years, in the seventh year you shall set that person free. And when you send a male slave out from you a free person, you shall not send him out empty-handed... Remember that you were a slave in the land of Egypt, and the LORD your God redeemed you; for this reason I lay this command upon you today.
DEUTERONOMY 15:12, 13, 15

A slave who deals wisely will rule over a child who acts shamefully, and will share the inheritance as one of the family.
PROVERBS 17:2

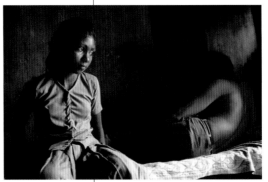

The modern evil of sex slavery. 14-year-old Rani has been working as a prostitute for a year. Her 'father' keeps all the money she earns. She is not his child, but was bought at the age of three.

Slavery in the New Testament

The apostle Paul stated a fundamental principle about the equality of all people 'in Christ': 'There is no longer Jew or Greek, there is no longer slave or free, there is no longer male and female; for all of you are one in Christ Jesus' (Galatians 3:28). However, in practice he accepted that slavery would continue and simply urged Christians to treat their slaves honourably – indeed, if they were Christians, to treat them as 'beloved brothers and sisters' (see Philemon verse 16). Christian slave-owners should not 'threaten' their slaves, knowing that 'both of you have the same Master in heaven, and with him there is no partiality' (Ephesians 6:9).

Having got the principle right, it still took the church about eighteen hundred years to recognize the equal rights of women, and almost the same length of time to work for the total abolition of slavery.

The Abolition Movement

When the emperor Constantine was converted he took on board Christian anxieties about the practice of slavery, and imperial legislation made for a considerable improvement in the conditions of slaves. Gradually this led to the disappearance of slavery in Christendom, to be replaced by the milder institution of serfdom (being tied to working on a particular estate), which in turn disappeared at the end of the Middle Ages.

However, from about that time the practice began of making slaves from 'native' people – many native Americans were enslaved in the 'colonies' by British, Spanish and Portuguese settlers and so were vast numbers of Africans who were transported to the Americas by boat. This trade was condemned by many missionaries and by successive popes, but it continued unabated until the eighteenth century, when the abolition movement began to gain wider support.

Christians and Abolition

The abolition movement was fuelled by stories gaining wide circulation in Europe and America of the appalling conditions on the slave boats transporting Africans to the colonies. Crammed below decks, without adequate food or clean water and with little or no sanitation, many didn't survive the dreadful journey. Led by the Quakers at first, who voiced their opposition on both sides of the Atlantic, Christians began to see this as a fundamental moral issue. In Europe the voice of the Catholic Church, which had condemned the practice of slavery while many Catholic countries continued to benefit from it economically, became stronger on the issue. If each individual human being is precious in the sight of God, which the Bible clearly teaches, what justification can there be for treating some as without value except as tools and implements of others? It was with arguments like this that William Wilberforce, in Britain, and men such as Henry Ward Beecher in the USA, and many others – almost all of them active Christians – pressed for the legal abolition of slavery. As early as 1793 John Graves, the governor of Upper Canada, banned the importation of slaves.

Wilberforce's Bill for abolition finally got through the British Parliament and became law in 1807. The issue was more sensitive in the USA, because most of the slaves were to be found in the Southern states, but finally in 1865 a constitutional amendment was passed prohibiting slavery anywhere in the United States for ever.

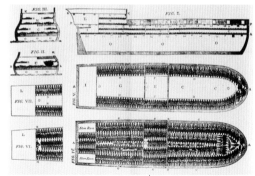

A print of a slave ship from 1789 shows the inhumanely cramped conditions.

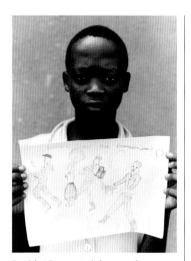

David, 15, spent eight months with the Lord's Resistance Army in Uganda, during which time he was forced to beat five people to death who had tried to escape. His drawing shows a captive being marched along by the rebels.

SLAVERY IN TODAY'S WORLD

Although slavery is prohibited by mandate of the United Nations, it is widely practised under various forms even in the modern world. Women are effectively sold into slavery in many of the world's great cities to work in brothels and sex clubs. They are 'slaves' because they did not agree to be used in this way and cannot escape from it. In some countries domestic servants are to all intents and purposes 'slaves' in that they do not receive a proper wage and are tied to the home where they work by sheer necessity. To be a slave is to live involuntarily under the absolute control of someone else, and in the nature of slavery there is no easy escape from it.

Cheap migrant labour in affluent lands is often operated outside the legal framework under what are virtually slave conditions: low wages, slum accommodation, long hours and no way of escape.

HARRIET BEECHER STOWE

Harriet Beecher Stowe was born in Connecticut, USA, in 1811. Her family were strongly opposed to slavery at a time when the issue was dividing Americans, Harriet's brother Henry being a leading figure in the abolitionist campaign. Most of the public persuasion was based on issues of morality or social good, but Harriet could see that powerful emotional arguments could be effective too. As a novelist, she took up the subject in her book *Uncle Tom's Cabin*, a homely and somewhat sentimental tale that opened the eyes of many ordinary Americans to what life was really like for the slaves who worked in the cotton fields of the Southern states. It

was published in 1850, and 15 years later slavery was finally and permanently abolished in the United States. She died in 1896, but the book has remained in print ever since.

Christianity and Race

Christianity was born into a world in which racial difference was critical. The Jews despised the Samaritans and feared the Romans, while Gentiles of all races were considered simply as pagans. In the Roman empire, which encompassed many different races and languages, there was a very clear pecking order, with those who held Roman citizenship at the very top of the pile. Society itself was layered: the aristocracy (the 'patricians') were the top layer; then the wealthy merchants; then the hard-working artisans; and finally, right at the bottom, were the slaves.

Yet into this unyielding mix of divisions, labels and discriminations came the Christians, proclaiming, as the apostle Paul did, that 'in Christ' there was 'neither Jew nor Greek, male nor female, slave nor free'. All were 'one in Christ Jesus'. So in one bold statement he dismissed some of the most impenetrable barriers of the ancient world: race, gender, class.

Through the centuries the church has struggled to remain true to this vision, and has often failed. Yet in the last century it has to be said that Christians have been in the forefront of the struggle to defeat the evil of racism – the judging of a person not by their character or behaviour, but by their race or the colour of their skin.

Christianity and Racism

Christians regard racism practised by an individual as a sin, and racism tolerated by a society as an evil, for these reasons:

1. Each human being is created equal in the sight of God, bears his image and is loved and valued by him.

2. God calls people of every race, tribe, language and culture to enter the kingdom of heaven (Revelation 7:9).

3. Among those races and tribes, God has no 'favourites' (Acts 10:34).

4. 'God so loved the *world* (literally, the "cosmos")' that he gave his only Son to save it. What God loves, his creatures should not despise.

Jesus and People of Other Races

Jesus said that his primary mission was to 'the lost sheep of the house of Israel', but he had several encounters with people of other races, religions and cultures, in all of which he responded positively to their needs. Among them were:

A Syro-Phoenician Woman: She asked Jesus to heal her daughter, but at first he refused. She persisted, falling to her knees and pleading for his help. He eventually responded with these words: 'Woman, great is your faith! Let it be done for you as you wish.' And her daughter was healed instantly (Matthew 15:21–24).

A Roman Centurion: This man came to Jesus to seek healing for his slave who was paralysed and in distress. Jesus offered to come to his house to see the slave, but the centurion said he wasn't 'worthy' for Jesus to come under his roof. 'Only speak the word, and my servant will be healed.' Jesus remarked that he had not found faith like that in Israel – and by speaking the word healed the slave (Matthew 8:5–13).

The Samaritan Leper: On one occasion Jesus healed ten men suffering from leprosy, but only one turned back to give thanks to God. He was a Samaritan, a race despised by the Jews (Luke 17:11–19).

THE CHURCH AND RACIAL DISTINCTION

From early days the Christian church was a truly open society. All baptized members were equal in the sight of God and 'drank from the same cup' at Communion – a truly revolutionary principle when it is considered that all social classes would have been among their number. Master and slave shared the cup together. Never before, as far as we can tell, anywhere in the world had there been a society as open and free as this one.

Issues of Racial Discrimination Today

While the Christian faith was largely confined to Europe there were problems of class distinction and vast inequalities of wealth, but racism was not a major issue. However, when Christian missions began to take the faith to Africa, India, Latin America and the Far East concepts of racial superiority and discrimination began to arise. Most of the missionaries were well-meaning, and often developed a genuine love and respect for the people among whom they worked, but they tended to treat them as children rather than as equals. On the heels of the missionaries came the slave-traders, who certainly didn't treat Africans with respect, but as commodities to be sold on the market.

Slavery was eventually abolished, but its legacy lingered on in the racial discrimination in America between 'whites' and 'blacks', mostly the descendants of slaves. In Africa some of the European colonial powers treated native Africans as second-class people – notably in South Africa, where apartheid (living apart) became the policy pursued by successive (white) governments.

During the last century Christians have led the world-wide struggle against racism, though Mahatma Gandhi (1869–1948), a Hindu, was one of the first to enunciate the principle of human rights where racial issues were concerned. He did this first while in South Africa as a young lawyer and then in India during the struggle for independence.

South Africa

South Africa became a focal point of concern during the 1950s and 60s, with the white government implementing its policy of apartheid and the black people, supported by white liberals and most of the churches, struggling to assert their rights. The black leader Nelson Mandela was imprisoned on Robben Island, only eventually being released when the battle was won and the nation became, in his words, 'Rainbow Coloured'. He was elected the new nation's first president.

Europe

When large-scale immigration to Europe from the Caribbean, East Africa and the Indian sub-continent occurred in the late 1950s and subsequently, 'racism' became a live issue, fuelled by anti-immigrant propaganda and violence on the streets of big cities.

The United States

In the USA black citizens, especially in some Southern states, were subject to 'segregation' – forced to use separate buses, beaches or public facilities. These and other human rights matters were taken up by a coalition of national church leaders, white liberals and the pastors of the black-led churches of the South. Notable among this last group was a Baptist minister, Martin Luther King Jr, who rapidly became the leader of the civil rights movement. In May 1954 the Supreme Court ruled that segregation was unlawful, though it took a long while to eliminate it. Martin Luther King was assassinated in 1968.

Armed South African police watch the procession of mourners carrying the banned African National Congress flag at the mass funeral of student activists shot by the police in Alexandra, South Africa, 1986.

Nelson Mandela revisits the cell at Robben Island prison where he was jailed for more than two decades, 1994.

Martin Luther King leading a march in Alabama to protest against the lack of voting rights for African Americans, March 1965.

Christianity and the Creation

CARING FOR THE WORLD

One of the great issues of the early twenty-first century has been human responsibility for the state of the planet. 'Global warming', caused by excessive carbon emissions, mostly of human origin, threatens to make life on earth more and more insecure, with the possibility of large-scale flooding as the ice-caps melt, failing crops as fertile land changes to desert, and extremes of temperature and wind even in the temperate areas of the planet.

These issues have of course exercised world governments and their scientific advisers, but the matter is as much one of individual responsibility as government action, which is why Christians have become deeply involved in the environmental movement. Global warming is largely the fruit of human prosperity. The richest nations, led by the USA, are the greatest polluters of the planet, and it is the demand for more and more goods and for greater personal mobility that fuels the problem. It is now widely recognized that the problem requires a major change of behaviour – indeed, of lifestyle – on the part of the public, who have generally been slow to see it as *their* problem. Faith groups have also been slow to take up the challenge, but since the millennium that has changed dramatically.

What the Bible Says About People and the Planet

So God created humankind in his image, in the image of God he created them; male and female he created them. God blessed them, and God said to them, 'Be fruitful and multiply, and fill the earth and subdue it; and have dominion over the fish of the sea and over the birds of the air and over every living thing that moves upon the earth.'... And it was so. God saw everything that he had made, and indeed, it was very good.
GENESIS 1:26, 31

When the writer of Genesis speaks of human beings 'subduing' the earth he certainly does not mean 'exploit' it. The word he used could equally be translated 'regulate' it – as the 'stewards' of creation humans bear the fearful responsibility of regulating or controlling the planet. This buck can't be passed to anyone else!

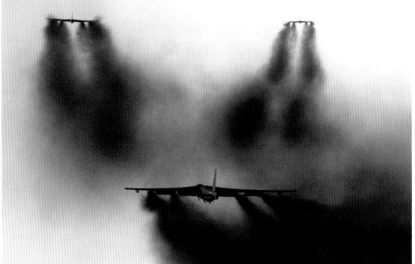

As three heavy bombers take off, they graphically illustrate one cause of the pollution of our planet.

The Bible and the Land

Six years you shall sow your field, and six years you shall prune your vineyard, and gather in their yield; but in the seventh year there shall be a sabbath of complete rest for the land, a sabbath for the Lord: you shall not sow your field or prune your vineyard.
LEVITICUS 25:3, 4

The land shall not be sold in perpetuity, for the land is mine; with me you are but aliens and tenants.
LEVITICUS 25:23

● SEE ALSO
THE CREATION AND THE
CREATOR P14-15

A Christian Approach to the Environment

1. The universe was created by God. He gives it meaning and purpose.

2. Everything that he creates is good, and to be respected. This includes humans, animals, birds, plant life and the earth itself.

3. Human beings are to regulate the earth as God's 'stewards' or agents, but will be held to account for their stewardship.

4. Greed, exploitation and indifference to the needs of others are personal sins and social evils.

5. Christians should support action to control excessive consumption, ensure a fair distribution of the earth's resources and avoid further damage to the eco-balance of the planet.

What People Have Said About the Environment

'The sun, the moon and the stars would have disappeared long ago had they happened to be within the reach of predatory human hands.'
HAVELOCK ELLIS

'There is a sufficiency in the world for man's need, but not for man's greed.'
MAHATMA GANDHI

'Such prosperity as we have known it up to the present is the consequence of rapidly spending the planet's irreplaceable capital.'
ALDOUS HUXLEY

'Everything is perfect coming from the hands of the Creator; everything degenerates in the hands of man.'
JEAN-JACQUES ROUSSEAU

'One is almost inclined to say that men are the devils on earth, and animals the tortured souls.'
ARTHUR SCHOPENHAUER

An empty storehouse. A small victim of a severe famine in the region of Ayod in southern Sudan. Human mismanagement of the planet makes it likely that such disasters will become more frequent.

Al Gore

AN INCONVENIENT TRUTH

An Inconvenient Truth is the title of a film-documentary written and presented by Al Gore, former vice-president of the USA and a Baptist. It won an Academy Award as best documentary of the year. The environment has been his passion since college days, but recently he has taken upon himself the role of chief and eloquent spokesperson for the environmental lobby in his country. He sees global warming as the 'inconvenient truth' – the one we don't want to face because it will cost us something in terms of comfort, luxury and lifestyle.

'Some of the leading scientists are now saying we may have as little as ten years before we cross a point of no return,' he warns. 'Beyond that point it's much more difficult to save the habitability of the planet in the future.'

Christianity and the State

GOD OR CAESAR?

Although Jesus had never attacked the Roman occupiers or recommended violence against them, his claim to some kind of kingly authority made him an object of political suspicion and in the end led to his death. In one way, that biblical scenario has set the scene for the long history of the relationship between the Christian church and the civil powers. While the church has gone along with the state, there has been little trouble. But when from time to time the church has felt it right to oppose the state, then open conflict, even persecution, has ensued.

From the earliest times Christian leaders have struggled with the dilemma of how to relate to the secular powers. The New Testament writers unanimously agree that Christians should be loyal citizens, pay their taxes and honour those in authority – and, indeed, pray for them (1 Timothy 2:1–3). On the other hand, when those civil powers demanded that Christians revere the emperor as divine, which in conscience they could not do, terrible persecution followed.

And still today, in a very different world, Christians feel themselves citizens of two jurisdictions: the 'kingdoms of this world' and the kingdom of heaven. Therein lies the tension...

What the New Testament Says About the State

Obey the Law

Let every person be subject to the governing authorities; for there is no authority except from God, and those authorities that exist have been instituted by God... Pay to all what is due them – taxes to whom taxes are due, revenue to whom revenue is due, respect to whom respect is due, honour to whom honour is due.
ROMANS 13:1, 7

Pray for the Rulers

First of all, then, I urge that supplications, prayers, intercessions, and thanksgivings be made for everyone, for kings and all who are in high positions, so that we may lead a quiet and peaceable life in all godliness and dignity.
1 TIMOTHY 2:1, 2

Honour the Emperor

For the Lord's sake accept the authority of every human institution, whether of the emperor as supreme, or of governors, as sent by him to punish those who do wrong and to praise those who do right... Honour everyone. Love the family of believers. Fear God. Honour the emperor.
1 PETER 2:13–17

Recognize a Higher Power

(The council of the high priest warned the apostles), 'We gave you strict orders not to teach in this name, yet here you have filled Jerusalem with your teaching and you are determined to bring this man's blood on us.'
But Peter and the apostles answered, 'We must obey God rather than any human authority.'
ACTS 5:28, 29

RENDER TO CAESAR...

(The Pharisees asked Jesus), 'Tell us, then, what you think. Is it lawful to pay taxes to Caesar, or not?' But Jesus, aware of their malice, said, 'Why are you putting me to the test, you hypocrites? Show me the coin used for the tax.' And they brought him a denarius. Then he said to them, 'Whose head is this, and whose title?' They answered, 'Caesar's.' Then he said to them, 'Give therefore to Caesar the things that are Caesar's, and to God the things that are God's.'
MATTHEW 22:17–21

Claudius Nero, emperor from 54 to 68 CE. He ordered the persecution of Christians in 64 CE following the great fire in Rome, and was probably responsible for the execution of both Paul and Peter.

The Holy Roman Empire

From about the seventh century almost the whole of western Europe became part of a massive religious empire, controlled from Rome and with the pope effectively its head of state. By his permission princes and kings ruled. The power of excommunication (being barred from receiving the sacrament) was a highly effective means of ensuring allegiance.

At the time of the Reformation, Luther was shielded by the power of some influential German princes, who were prepared to ignore Rome's instructions; and in England Henry VIII rejected papal authority over his own highly irregular matrimonial arrangements, thus freeing the church to accept many principles and practices of the Continental Reformers. The French Revolution in the eighteenth century and the general growth of libertarian ideas in Europe finally buried the notion of a unified Christian state encompassing most of the Continent.

Christianity and Communism

The Russian Revolution in 1917 introduced a new kind of 'persecution' for the Christian church. Believers weren't fed to the lions, but they were subjected to enormous social and political pressures: churches were closed and it was forbidden to teach the Christian faith to anyone under sixteen. Some Christian activists were put in prison. The clear intention of the Communists was the gradual elimination of religion ('the opium of the people', in the words of Karl Marx) from the life of the nation.

A woman pauses at the memorial grave in front of the wall at Zimmerstrasse, Berlin, 1986.

A similar, though harsher, approach to religion, and especially Christianity, was adopted in China after the Revolution of 1949. Churches were forced to register with the state or be closed, pressure was put on them to adapt their message to the 'new' status quo, and those who did not conform were ruthlessly punished.

From 1985 onwards, as the Communists gradually lost power, the situation improved for Christians in Russia, with the Orthodox Church being accorded 'primacy' under a law of 1997. Some Protestant groups, however, have still suffered harassment. Things have also improved somewhat in China, though the churches are still heavily regulated by the state.

Separation of Church and State

The American Fathers and the French Revolutionaries were united in one thing: church and state should be separate and apart. The US Constitution enshrined the principle, as did the Constitution of Napoleonic France. Other nations followed, so that the idea of the 'secular state' – even in profoundly religious countries like the USA or India – became widely recognized. In the United Kingdom England and Scotland continued to have 'established' churches, largely in a symbolic or ceremonial role. In practice government is firmly in the hands of the state.

Other countries – Ireland and Spain, for instance – gave the Roman Catholic Church a recognized role in the culture of the nation, though no actual power in terms of government. A similar situation exists in many countries of eastern Europe, including Russia, where the Orthodox Church is recognized as the 'default' religion of the country.

Thomas Jefferson, third president of the United States, argued for the separation of church and state.

What People Have Said About Government

'It is very easy to accuse a government of imperfection, for all mortal things are full of it.'
MICHEL DE MONTAIGNE

'Christianity introduced no new forms of government, but a new spirit which totally transformed the old ones.'
JOHN ACTON

'Democracy is the very child of Jesus' teachings of the infinite worth of every personality.'
FRANCIS J. MCCONNELL

'No matter how noble the objectives of a government, if it blurs decency and human kindness, cheapens human life, and breeds ill will and suspicion – it is an evil government.'
ERIC HOFFER

Christianity in the Modern World
A WORLD-WIDE FAITH

Christianity in the twenty-first century is a genuinely world-wide religion in the sense that there is an active Christian presence in every one of the world's nations. The centre of Christian influence has shifted over the last century, with the 'new' churches of Africa, Latin America and Asia providing the cutting edge of Christian mission. In the West, apart from America, church membership has declined, and in a few Muslim lands the Christian church has to operate in a discreetly unobtrusive way; yet even in Communist North Korea and the People's Republic of China there are flourishing Christian churches.

The church of the twenty-first century is, and will doubtless increasingly become, a servant church, concerned with issues of justice, reconciliation and hope, and reminding an increasingly technological world that human beings are body, mind and spirit.

NORTH AMERICA

In many ways North America, and especially the USA, is the 'power-house' of modern Christianity. In 1973 it was calculated that 70 per cent of all Protestant missionaries in the world, and an even higher proportion of the total cost of missions, came from North America. As indigenous leadership has taken over in most lands, the number of missionaries may have dropped, but the dependence on American funds is still a problem facing churches that wish to be seen as truly independent. On the other hand, these statistics show the amazing vitality and commitment of American Christians who see that the message of Christ is for the whole world, not just the privileged West. Active church attendance in the USA is higher than anywhere else in the Western world but it seems to have peaked around the millennium. Numbers may be static, but the churches aren't, and Americans continue to volunteer in large numbers for Christian work in other lands.

SOUTH AMERICA

Roman Catholic missions, in the wake of the conquering Spanish armies, evangelized much of Latin America in the sixteenth and seventeenth centuries. Thus today the majority of people in South America are at least nominally Catholic. The church was energized in the twentieth century by the impact of Liberation Theology, an approach to Christianity that seeks to root belief in the actual day-to-day experience of people, especially the poor. The church hierarchy was unsure about the movement and some of its leaders were disciplined, but Gustavo Gutierrez, Juan Luis Segundo and the Boff brothers, among others, were recognized as major theological figures. Liberation Theology also had its Protestant counterparts, but it was Pentecostalism that made the greatest impact in the late twentieth century, with many former Roman Catholics joining their churches.

A bishop reading scriptures in the church of the Abuna Garima monastery, Tigray, Ethiopia.

AFRICA

The continent of Africa south of the Sahara is generally regarded as the scene of the church's most vigorous recent growth. Today the churches planted by missionaries in the previous centuries are now all under national leadership, though retaining their earlier denominational links. These traditional churches are probably outnumbered by indigenous ones, which reflect African culture and lifestyle. There are significant Christian minorities in some of the Muslim lands in the north, especially Egypt, Ethiopia and Morocco. In the southern two-thirds of Africa, Christianity is the dominant religion. Church congregations are large and the services lengthy! African Christianity has produced some outstanding leaders, including Nobel prize-winner Desmond Tutu.

WESTERN EUROPE

Although this is often described as a 'post-Christian' era in Europe because in most countries active church membership is low, most of the population describe themselves as 'Christian', and there are vigorous and growing churches to be found in every country of the continent. Active church membership is probably strongest in a few traditionally Catholic countries, notably Ireland, Spain, Italy and Portugal, and in Orthodox Greece. In the predominantly Protestant areas, such as the United Kingdom, northern Germany and Scandinavia, active church membership has probably stabilized, but there are many growing churches all over western Europe, mostly of an evangelical or charismatic style.

EASTERN EUROPE

Since the collapse of Communism, the lands of eastern Europe have in many cases rediscovered their historic Christian faith, whether Orthodox, Roman Catholic or Reformed. In countries such as Poland the majority of people are practising Christians and the churches are crowded for Sunday mass. In Russia the Orthodox Church has reasserted its influence and is regarded as embodying the 'spirit of Russia'. This resurgence of Christianity in eastern Europe is not without its problems, especially where the large Islamic enclaves in the Balkans and elsewhere are concerned.

ASIA

The greater part of the world's population lives in Asia, much of it in the People's Republic of China and in India. Although there has been Christian missionary work throughout Asia for at least six hundred years, it was only in the twentieth century that the Christian faith established a genuinely indigenous ('native') foothold in the continent. For the most part, sticking to their religious heritage, the people of Asia are Buddhist, Hindu or Muslim, though the prevailing 'faith' in China and North Korea is, of course, atheism. However, there is a vigorous and growing Christian church in South Korea, with perhaps a third of the population claiming to be active Christians, and all the evidence is that in China the churches, whether registered or unregistered, are experiencing rapid growth. There are substantial Christian minorities in India (especially in the south), Indonesia (though under enormous pressure from militant Islamic groups), Sri Lanka and Vietnam. Indeed, every country in Asia has at least a Christian presence, and in countries like Japan there is a great deal of interest in Christianity as a way of life.

Boys light devotional candles at the Basilica del Santo Niño in Cebu City, Philippines.

THE PACIFIC AND AUSTRALASIA

As one might expect, the story of Christianity in Australia and New Zealand is largely that of European immigration, though the native people of the lands, the 'Aborigines' and the Maoris, have eventually been welcomed not only into membership but also leadership in the Christian church. Christianity is strong, though probably static in terms of active membership, in these countries, as it is in most of the Pacific islands (Papua New Guinea, Tonga, Fiji, Hawaii and the Philippines, and many smaller ones). However, Australia and New Zealand have played a major role in mission and support work in the Pacific area.

The Cathedral of St Paul surrounded by office blocks in the central business district of Melbourne, Australia.

Christianity and the Future
'THE BRAVE NEW WORLD'

For the first Christians there was no 'future' in terms of earthly life. Jesus had said that he would come back, and they lived as though that might happen at any moment. Planning for the future would be a sheer waste of time: there wasn't going to *be* any. Slowly the early church realized that there had been no prediction by Jesus as to *when* this Second Coming would be – quite the contrary. He had said that even he didn't know when it would be; it was presumptuous to assume that it would take place before most of the people in the world had had an opportunity to hear about Jesus and believe. So we find the apostle Paul warning the Christians at Thessalonica not to give up their jobs or live in idleness, as some were doing, in expectation of the imminent end of all things.

Two thousand years later, it could be said that Christians are *still* waiting, but they realize that their task is to live now, in the present, and to relate the story of Jesus to the world in which they live – a very different one from that of the first century. So modern Christians are living in the 'in-between' – after the days when Jesus was on earth, and before the day when (in some probably unimaginable way) he will 'return'. They have an 'old' message, but a new audience. To relate the one to the other is probably the greatest task facing Christianity in the twenty-first century.

A CLASH OF VALUES	
Modern 'Western' values	**Traditional Christian values**
Prosperity	Simplicity
Status	Humility
Health	Wholeness
Style	Modesty
Success	Service

Reflection of the spire of St Martin's Church in the facade of the Bullring shopping centre at Birmingham, England.

● See Also
THE FINAL VICTORY P26-27

Visions of the Future

The Hebrew prophets and the writer of Revelation in the New Testament offer many wonderful visions of a future of peace, prosperity and joy.

The End of Warfare

He shall judge between the nations, and shall arbitrate for many peoples; they shall beat their swords into ploughshares, and their spears into pruning hooks; nation shall not lift up sword against nation, neither shall they learn war any more.
ISAIAH 2:4

The Wasteland Renewed

Thus says the Lord: In this place of which you say, 'It is a waste without human beings or animals,' in the towns of Judah and the streets of Jerusalem that are desolate, without inhabitants, human or animal, there shall once more be heard the voice of mirth and the voice of gladness, the voice of the bridegroom and the voice of the bride, the voices of those who sing, as they bring thank offerings to the house of the LORD.
JEREMIAH 33:10, 11

No Tears, No Pain

And I heard a loud voice from the throne saying, 'See, the home of God is among mortals. He will dwell with them as their God; they will be his peoples, and God himself will be with them; he will wipe every tear from their eyes. Death will be no more; mourning and crying and pain will be no more, for the first things have passed away.'
REVELATION 21:3, 4

'To have a special concern for the poor' – victims of the Asian tsunami of 2004 queue for food at a maksehift refugee camp in Sri Lanka.

What People Have Said About the Future

'*Most people prefer and strive for the present, we for the future.*'
ST AMBROSE OF MILAN

'*He that fears not the future may enjoy the present.*'
THOMAS FULLER

'*The only light upon the future is faith.*'
THEODOR HOECKER

'*You can never plan the future by the past.*'
EDMUND BURKE

'*The best thing about the future is that it only comes one day at a time.*'
ABRAHAM LINCOLN

Cotton canopies are used to protect young tomato plants from the searing heat of the Jordan Valley, Israel.

A Manifesto for the Modern Church

1. To live simply, that others may simply live (Luke 6:20).

2. To be open, welcoming and inclusive as a community and generous as individuals (Ephesians 4:32).

3. To share with people everywhere the good news of Jesus, but to do it with sensitivity and respect (1 Peter 3:15, 16).

4. To strive for the goals of God's 'kingdom': justice, joy and peace (Romans 14:17).

5. To have a special concern for the marginalized in our societies: the poor, the exploited, the sick and the weak (Galatians 2:10).

6. To make its worship, its words and its work relevant to contemporary life (1 Corinthians 14:23–25).

7. To be the 'salt' that gives life flavour; the 'light' that shows the way; and the 'new wine' that brings joy to the world (Matthew 5:14–16; Luke 5:37).

Index

Index

Picture acknowledgments

Alamy: pp. 12 Church Mouse Photography; 13c, 39l, 65al Israel Images; 13r, 33a, 76, 96b Mary Evans Picture Library; 14 Derek Croucher; 15b, 121b mediacolor's; 16r, 40a, 46b, 67bl, 78, 91br The London Art Archive; 17 David Pearson; 22 Leslie Garland Picture Library; 25a, 92b World Religions Photo Library; 29al David Wootton; 36 Lionel Derimais; 37a Kim Karpeles; 38, 67bm, 72b Interfoto Pressebildagentur; 42b Martin Shields; 43 imagebroker; 46a, 63b ArkReligion.com; 47m Pontino; 47b Simon Hadley; 48b Chris Willson; 49a, 64, 67br, 80b, 86, 98b,103b The Print Collector; 51r Martin Norris; 53a Jeff Morgan religion; 55b, 91bl Michael Juno; 60a LondonPhotos – Homer Sykes; 62 Robert Harding Picture Library Ltd; 63a IML Image Group Ltd; 65ar Jon Arnold Images Ltd; 66 Roger Coulam; 68a Hemis; 69 CuboImages srl; 70b Shein Audio Visual; 77r Richard Baker; 79a David Hancock; 80a, 97a Lebrecht Music and Arts Photo Library; 91a Images&Stories; 93a CountrySideCollection – Homer Sykes; 94 Gregory Wrona; 97m Peter Titmuss; 97b World History Archive; 98a vario images GmbH & Co.KG; 99a isafa Image Service s.r.o.; 99b Jason Hosking; 100a Classic Image; 104 Trevor Booth Photography; 106 Bill Varie; 108a North Wind Picture Archives; 112, 123 Mike Goldwater; 119l Stockfolio; 120 Borderlands; 121r Worldfoto; 122 Joe Tree

Art Archive: pp. 15ar Bibliothèque Municipale Moulins/Gianni Dagli Orti; 23 Cenacolo Santa Apollonia Florence/Gianni Dagli Orti; 26 Museo Correr Venice/Alfredo Dagli Orti; 27a Scrovegni Chapel Padua/Gianni Dagli Orti; 27b Sucevita Monastery Moldavia Romania/ Alfredo Dagli Orti; 42a Galleria d'Arte Moderna Rome/Alfredo Dagli Orti; 48a Museo Franz Mayer Mexico/Gianni Dagli Orti; 54 Voronet Monastery Moldavia Romania/Alfredo Dagli Orti; 84 Episcopal Museum Vic Catalonia/Gianni Dagli Orti; 87r National Gallery London/Eileen Tweedy; 88 Scrovegni Chapel Padua/Alfredo Dagli Orti; 95r Museo del Prado Madrid; 95bl Gemaldegalerie Dresden; 111a Bibliothèque Municipale Bar-sur-Aube/Gianni Dagli Orti; 111b Museo Civico San Gimignano/Alfredo Dagli Orti

Corbis: pp. 28a, 41 Kazuyoshi Nomachi; 29b Philippe Lossac/Godong; 29ar, 30b Corbis; 31br JP Laffont/Sygma; 37br David Turnley; 38-39 National Gallery Collection; 40b Francis G. Mayer; 56r Richard T. Nowitz; 58, 118 Araldo de Luca; 60 Alessandra Benedetti; 74 Kevin Fleming; 75b, 77al Bettmann; 79b Elder Neville; 83b Sophie Elbaz/Sygma; 85b Bernd Settnik/ epa; 89a Julio Donoso; 89b Dean Conger; 90a Annie Griffiths Belt; 103a Laszlo Balogh/ Reuters; 107l, 110 Underwood & Underwood; 108b Pierre Perrin/Sygma; 109a Stefano Bianchetti; 109b Andrew Lichtenstein; 115m Louise Gubb; 115a Gideon Mendel; 115b Steve Schapiro; 117al Jon Jones/Sygma

Hanan Isachar: p. 85a

Lion Hudson: pp. 13l David Townsend; 90b Nicholas Rous

David Alexander: pp. 18, 53b

Getty Images: pp. 18, 20r, 31ar, 35a, 87l AFP; 20l, 77bl, 77bm, 107r, 116a, 117br, 123 Getty; 21, 57, 60b, 75a, 101, 113a The Bridgeman Art Library; 28b, 45al Axiom RM; 30a Penny Tweedle; 31al Joe McNally; 32 Philip & Karen Smith; 33b Benjamin Shearn; 34 Annie Griffiths Belt; 35b Christopher Pillitz; 37bl Per-Anders Pettersson; 44b Aurora Creative; 45ar Ross M. Horowitz; 47a popperfoto; 49b John Borthwick; 51l Sami Sarkis; 55a Tony May; 56l, 70a National Geographic Creative; 58-59 Siegfried Layda; 65b, 71 Gallo Images; 72a Nabeel Turner; 73 Panoramic Images; 81a Lonely Planet Images; 81b VCL/Spencer Rowell; 83a, 113br Time & Life Pictures; 100b Science Faction; 113bl Andy Sewell; 116b Visuals Unlimited; 119r Eric Van Den Brulle

Jon Arnold Images: pp. 44a, 102

Andy Rous: p. 93b

Photolibrary: pp. 39, 45b, 49m, 67al, 68b

Scala: pp. 24 © 2004, Photo Pierpont Morgan Library/Art Resource; 25b, 95a, 105 1990, Photo Scala, Florence

Zev Radovan: pp. 8, 11, 16bl, 17a, 92a, 96a

Lion Hudson

Commissioning editor:
Kate Kirkpatrick

Project editors: Catherine Sinfield, Miranda Powell

Proofreader: Rachel Ashley-Pain (freelancer)

Designer: Nicholas Rous

Picture researchers: Nicholas Rous, Kate Leech, Jenny Ward

Production manager: Kylie Ord